Command

Performance

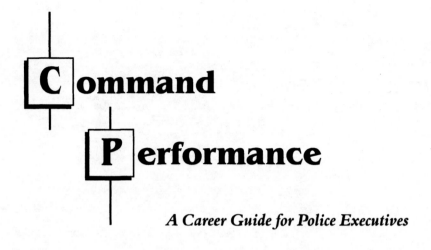

Command

Performance

A Career Guide for Police Executives

By
William E. Kirchhoff
Charlotte Lansinger
and
James Burack

POLICE EXECUTIVE
RESEARCH FORUM

Printed in the United States of America

Library of Congress Number 99-75128

ISBN 1-878734-68-7

Cover by Marnie Deacon Kenney

⊤able of Contents

F oreword

I VIVIDLY REMEMBER the telephone call, even though it was nearly 15 years ago. I was in a New England snowstorm on a police chief selection trip and called my Washington, D.C., office to check my messages. One was from a police chief who had been referred by a mutual friend. My assistant said the message was urgent. From a telephone booth, with snow flying, I called the chief. A career police executive, he had just been given his walking papers by the city. He explained his predicament—he was married, with a mortgage, two children and the holidays fast approaching. The anxiety in his voice was unmistakable. He said he had never been jobless and the prospect of seeking work in the only profession he knew—policing—was daunting. He had never compiled a résumé, written a cover letter, or interviewed in a competitive process. He had little sense of what to do to get another position and he was looking for a place to turn for advice. He was desperate.

As we talked through his situation and devised a short-term strategy, he became calmer and more confident about his prospects. And it occurred to me that there should be a better way to help aspiring and incumbent chiefs prepare for law enforcement executive positions and sudden career changes. As similar calls increased over the years, I recognized that there was a need for a publication offering that type of information. Nearly every day I speak to a police chief considering a new position, or a command-level police manager aspiring to be a chief. These are people committed to their communities who want to advance public safety but need information on how to go about finding the right position, and successfully competing. Each time I speak with someone searching for information, I wish there were a book I might recommend to them that would assist them in their careers. At long last, here is a compilation of some outstanding advice that will benefit present and future police leaders.

Along the way I met Bill Kirchhoff, then city manager of Arlington, Texas. Bill is a unique person who immediately grasped the need to help aspiring police executives move up the career ladder. During his time as a city manager in Arlington, and before that in Colorado and Illinois, he hired numerous police chiefs and gained a reputation as one of the most knowledgeable city managers in the country on what it takes to succeed as a police executive. He began to teach seminars on the subject, and wrote a book called *How Bright Is Your Badge,* which he readily photocopied and distributed for no cost when requested. The book explained the police chief selection process and the qualities required to be a successful police executive. News of the book was passed by word-of-mouth among aspiring police executives, commanders, and officers. Kirchhoff received a steady stream of requests from them for the publication.

Over the years, as requests for copies of the book increased, Bill asked me if PERF would be willing to update and revise his initial effort and publish it as a PERF book. I enthusiastically said yes, knowing that this book would provide useful information for many police leaders searching for career guidance. Charlotte Lansinger, who came with me to PERF some six years ago, and has significant experience in administering police chief search processes and routinely dispensing career advice to chiefs, took on a major role in rewriting and updating Kirchhoff's initial effort. I also was fortunate to be able to call on Jim Burack to take a leading role in the production of the book. Jim had been a police officer in Westminster, Colo., and then went on to law school and became a U.S. Marine Corps prosecutor, before coming to PERF as legal counsel, director of operations and an associate in police executive searches.

They, with the assistance of many other PERF staff and consultants over the past couple of years, have expanded the scope of the book beyond what Bill and I originally envisioned. From a comprehensive survey of police chiefs (cited in a front-page story in the *New York Times*) overseen by Jim Burack, to discussions with countless chiefs, to calling on leading police thinkers such as Herman Goldstein, Egon Bittner, George Kelling, Mary Ann Wycoff, Ed Flynn, Bob Wasserman and Lawrence Sherman for advice and counsel, PERF staff have developed a book that provides both a practical and academic perspective on career development for police executives.

This book is foremost a review of the police chief selection process aimed primarily at those police executives who want to make an impact on policing and advance professionally. Not everyone who reads *Command Performance* will choose to go on to become a police chief, but it should nonetheless prove extremely valuable to every police professional. From deciding whether one wants to be a police executive to researching potential career opportunities, from career planning to the obstacle course-like selection process— including writing a résumé, crafting a persuasive cover letter, interviewing, and finally, negotiating a satisfactory compensation package—this book takes the reader through the process in a systematic way, providing a roadmap for prospective police executives to devise a winning strategy.

The intention of this book is not only to help individual careers, but ultimately to better prepare our most promising police executives to compete successfully for leadership positions and consequently improve public safety for communities across this country and around the world. Local government officials and hiring authorities will find the book helpful in developing internal career development programs to provide opportunities for advancement and avoid losing rising stars to other agencies. And as I look back on the telephone call I received some 15 years ago, I hope that in addition to providing informal advice and moral support, *Command Performance* will be a useful desk reference for a chief as he or she prepares for the future.

My appreciation goes to my friend and colleague, Bill Kirchhoff, for allowing us to expand on his vision and to Charlotte Lansinger, Jim Burack, the many PERF staff members and consultants, and police executives who played a role in developing this book—a genuine resource for police leaders in the 21st century.

Chuck Wexler
Executive Director
Police Executive Research Forum
Washington, D.C.

A cknowledgements

C OUNTLESS INDIVIDUALS have contributed to the insights that are shared in this book. From both successful and unsuccessful job candidates whose résumés we have reviewed, to many we have met in interviews, to the employers we have worked with during the selection processes, many people unwittingly and without intention contributed to this book.

The PERF staff, consultants and police executives contributed to this book in many ways. Chuck Wexler was the impetus behind this book—explaining the vision and bringing staff together to complete the project. He also supplied invaluable editorial additions and suggestions. Ellen Dollar showed expert editorial ability and great patience in editing the entire manuscript and making many substantive suggestions. Martha Plotkin ensured that production continued to move forward. Jane Marcin played a critical role in shepherding the drafts from authors to editors and back, and updating reference information. Richard and Tom Burack assisted in editing early drafts of the book. Antionette Means, Audrey Peterbark and Kevin Haggerty all assisted with various editorial tasks. We owe a special thanks to Chief Ed Flynn of Arlington, Virginia, for his editorial comments, and to all of the police executives who allowed us to use their résumés as samples.

A key resource cited throughout the book is PERF's 1997 survey of police executives. PERF staff, including, Anne Grant, research associate; Lisa Shores, PERF fellow and sergeant with the Charlotte-Mecklenburg, N.C., Police Department; Tom Baker and Steve Dourney, interns; and John Kennedy, consultant, were instrumental in completing the survey.

We compiled the suggested reading list by consulting with a number of prominent sources around the country. Reaching complete consensus on the best in police literature would be impossible, but Egon Bittner, Herman Goldstein, Bob Lunney, Lawrence Sherman, Ron Glensor, Mary Ann Wycoff and Bob Wasserman, among others, made suggestions for sources to include. The staff of the International City/County Management Association's Retirement Corporation was helpful in providing information on compensation and benefits issues.

Finally, we have made every effort to ensure the information contained in this volume is up-to-date and accurate. However, if an error has crept in, the fault lies with us, the authors, and not with the contributors recognized above.

William E. Kirchhoff

Charlotte Lansinger

James Burack

1 | Getting a Job in a Competitive Market

SOUND ADVICE for the law enforcement professional who wants to be a police chief, or a chief who wants to advance to a better position, is hard to come by. Literature on the subject is thin, because there are relatively few people who know much about it. It is abundantly clear that most police chief aspirants are not well prepared to compete for jobs outside their agencies.

Command Performance: A Career Guide for Police Executives covers issues such as career planning, résumé writing, interview preparation, compensation package negotiation, employment agreements, use of executive search consultants, the importance of image, and other elements related to a successful police chief job search. It is an attempt to bring both potential and practicing police chiefs up to date on the law enforcement executive job market and provide information that will help them compete for the job they want.

The Police Executive Research Forum (PERF) conducted a survey in late 1997 of appointed police chiefs of the 500 largest city and county police agencies in the country. The collected data, covering topics such as selection, qualifications and benefits, represent the most comprehensive effort in the past 15 years to collect information about police chiefs from cities of more than 50,000 population. We will draw on that material throughout the book, and will refer to it as "PERF's survey" or "the PERF survey."

This book focuses on the two most basic questions a chief candidate should ask him- or herself: How do I best prepare to be a police chief? And having obtained the appropriate background, experience and training, how do I best compete in the chief selection process? The book offers insights on the job hunting aspect of career advancement. It suggests ways a person can more likely succeed in attaining the job of his or her choice. It also will identify the necessary tools of the trade that should be negotiated in advance to help you keep the job.

A Tough Profession

Not everyone is cut out to be a police chief. Depending on the circumstances, being a police chief can be exhilarating, or a constant battle. To survive is triumph enough for many. Chiefs are met with daily challenges

1

to their professional skills, emotional well-being and personal lives. Police chiefs deal in an environment where there is little common ground among competing constituencies who exert pressure on the chief.

The job is made more difficult by the public's general misperception of the business of policing, which frequently leads to unrealistic expectations of what a police chief can do. Much of a chief's work cannot be rehearsed or scripted, because there is no complete codifiable body of expertise that tells police chiefs what to do, and how to do it. Different constituencies have different expectations. On the other hand, there are few jobs that offer as many rewards as the job of police chief, even though many of those rewards are more intangible than monetary.

With full knowledge that police chiefs are routinely pressured by activist groups, beleaguered by politicians, and challenged by aggressive police organizations, just about everybody with a badge dreams of becoming the chief. But what will make you stand out from the rest of the pack? How strong are your qualifications? How significant is your experience? What are your chances? What is your capacity to respond to the challenge? In short, do you have the right stuff to be a chief?

Education

It is rare for chief candidates to successfully compete in any open search process without holding a bachelor's degree. Indeed, PERF's survey found that nearly nine in 10 chiefs hold a bachelor's degree.

This trend is driven by several factors, not the least being the ever-increasing professionalization of law enforcement. It is also influenced by the increased educational achievements of other police and city employees. It is not surprising that some jurisdictions with high populations of college-educated residents, or communities with institutions of higher learning, require a police chief to possess a college degree. Some communities prefer more advanced degrees. Indeed, a postgraduate degree is now becoming standard. PERF's survey indicated that about half of all major agency chiefs held an advanced degree (master's degree: 46.4%, doctorate: 1.4%, law: 3.4%).

Training obtained from reputable management programs can also be helpful. Widely recognized programs include the FBI's National Academy, Law Enforcement Executive Development Seminar (LEEDS) and National Executive Institute (NEI); PERF's Senior Management Institute for Police; Northwestern University Traffic Institute's School of Staff and Command; Harvard University's Program for Senior Executives in

State and Local Government; and Southern Police Institute's Administrative Officers Course. Other programs are more prominent regionally, such as those offered at Johns Hopkins University in Baltimore, Pennsylvania State University, development programs offered through the California POST, and many others.

Experience

Cities are looking for a chief who has had substantial experience managing a police organization, or directing a significant portion of an organization. Thus, police chiefs, deputy chiefs and division commanders are the most competitive candidates. Some of the best applicants for a mid-sized department possess experience as a chief in a smaller city, or have served as an assistant or deputy chief in a midsized agency. Applicants in the mid-management rank, even with experience in a major city police department, will find it difficult to compete with the anticipated candidate pool. Ultimately, the successful candidate should have significant *command* (not simply supervisory) experience. Command experience is considered operational responsibility for a specific area such as patrol, investigations or administration. It may also mean having overall responsibility for a geographic area, such as a precinct or district command.

There is no experience that completely grooms one for being the chief. Ultimately the best training to become a chief is to be a chief. No one knows whether or not he or she can take charge of a department until given the opportunity to do so. Taking charge means establishing mastery of the organization and influence over its people. Within a short time, new chiefs will have to move from the period when they are on the edge of their seats—when everything is anxiety producing—to making the machine run smoothly. If he or she cannot effect this transition, life as a police chief will be less than rewarding.

Background and situational factors influence a senior police commander's potential for success as well as failure. All too often, the organizational environment that surrounds a police commander is not conducive to or beneficial in the transition to the position of chief. Many individuals who wish to become chiefs rarely contemplate the differences between what they do currently, and what the chief does.

Senior police commanders make recommendations, are generally task-oriented, work in the present, are responsible for only a part of an organization, contend with internal politics, and make things happen. But the chief must make the final decision, be goal-oriented, work in the future, deal with the whole, be oriented toward concepts, face the challenge of external politics, and serve as the agency's planner. Because only some of what typical senior police commanders do prepares them for the chief's position, it is not surprising that they sometimes fail when they become chiefs.

There is a popular misconception that the chief runs the police department, enjoying complete autonomy. This could not be farther from the truth. Many groups with different interests contribute to the police chief's agenda. The effective police chief must be able to work with different groups of people, often having competing agendas—the media, politicians, judges, prosecutors, corrections officials, civic leaders, union representatives, clergy, and other special interest groups. Few can do this successfully. Only those police executives capable of dealing with the public and the press, scarce budget funds, and the realities of local politics are successful. It is an extremely difficult transition to move from the rigid, yet relatively comfortable, paramilitary bureaucracy of a police department into the more abstract arena where a police chief must operate.

To be effective and successful, the contemporary police chief must be a tactful diplomat, innovator, problem solver, team player, and leader, and must possess an energetic, positive and enthusiastic personality. He or she must possess qualities that go beyond education and experience.

Characteristics, Skills and Abilities: The "Right Stuff"

In his book about the early astronauts and test pilots, Thomas Wolfe talks about "the right stuff." Few can define it. But if police chiefs are going to achieve the job satisfaction they want, the recognition they desire, professional progress, and material advancement, they must be supplied with plenty of the "right stuff."

Leadership: Leadership is not a question of having power over subordinates, but of having influence with them. Many can manage, but few can lead. Right or wrong, successful police agencies are headed up by leader-managers, not manager-administrators.

Communication Skills: The most important relationship for you to establish as a newly appointed police chief is with your boss. Being able to communicate effectively with your boss can make the difference between a misunderstanding that gets worked out over lunch and one that gets you fired. A critical element of a chief's success is having a clear understanding of the manager's expectations. A positive relationship will help to ensure that these expectations are clearly communicated and understood. Effective communication skills are equally essential to establishing positive relationships with department personnel and the community.

Administrative and Management Skills: Balancing numerous projects, understanding budgeting, gathering input, and informing various constituencies are among the requirements for a good chief. An effective leader is measured by how well his or her strategies and programs are managed and incorporated into department operations to produce a good outcome.

Interpersonal Skills: The ability to be professional, friendly and compassionate can go a long way toward ensuring solid relationships with department personnel, the administration and the community.

Openness to Innovation and Progressive Change: Policing has not been a static field over the past 30 years. It has improved largely because of chiefs who were willing to experiment and remain open-minded to new developments.

Tangible Accomplishments: The ability to point to prior substantive and measurable successes is frequently a requirement to be seriously considered for a chief's position.

Team Player with Ability to Delegate Responsibility: Leaders have to know their subordinates and play to their strengths. You need to know what your subordinates are capable of handling.

Enthusiastic and Energetic Morale Builder: An effective chief is a cheerleader, capable of rallying support and convincing officers to be productive and professional, and the community to be an active partner with the police.

Integrity: An executive position requires uncompromised character and honesty in dealings with department personnel, city administration and the community.

Professional Confidence and Experience: This means you know your business and everybody else knows you know your business. Police professionals must know the business of policing better than anyone else. As policing becomes more and more professional, there is an increasing body of knowledge, of everything from crime trends to effective personnel management, with which police executives are expected to be familiar.

Intuition: Successful chiefs have strong intuition. You should be able to sense a change in the winds and be prepared to react.

Sense of Fairness and Equity: Chiefs are evaluated largely on their ability to make judicious and impartial decisions, and the degree of fairness with which they rate and direct subordinates.

A Catalyst for Change: You can count on two things among the uncertainties of the organization you manage—it will be different than it was in the past and different from what you expected it to be. Creativity and innovation are necessary for the chief's survival.

Partnership Building: Partnerships must be established with community leaders, elected officials, other department heads and your peers in the police profession. The ability to develop partnerships is critical to success, and failure to do so is often the primary reason for a chief's downfall.

Ability to Handle Sensitive Personnel Matters: You cannot manage a police department without having to either discipline or fire people. While there is a tendency to duck this task because it is unpleasant, it has to be done. When to do it, how to do it and how to gain the necessary support for your decisions are critical elements of successful personnel management.

A Strong Ego and Self-Confidence: The media, your officers, city council, labor organizations and the public will critically judge your actions on a daily basis. Without a strong ego and self-confidence, a chief can be debilitated by stress and insecurity.

Tenacious Worker: Little can do more for your reputation than hard work, and little can hurt you more than a lack of effort.

Toughness: The toughness required is not mean-spirited, but a spirit of resiliency.

Physical Capability: Police chiefs generally must be capable of carrying out the physical demands required of a police officer. A candidate must be minimally capable, in good health, and may be required to take a physical exam.

The Role of the Appointing Authority

Every city manager and mayor will differ somewhat on the profile he or she desires in a police chief, but there are some common elements that drive the selection of candidates. In one sense, both mayors and city managers want a police chief who can make law enforcement problems go away. There is a tendency, however, for mayors to select a police chief on the basis of political realities, while city managers are more inclined to use efficiency and administrative competence as the selection benchmarks. And while neither is right or wrong, police chief aspirants need to recognize that there will most likely be a difference in the organizational environment of a city in which the chief executive is appointed (usually called a city manager), and one where the chief executive is elected (typically a mayor).

There are a number of attributes that make up a law enforcement executive's qualifications—education and training, rank and experience, professional reputation and contacts. Character and personality, as well as "fit" are equally important. As qualified as one might be on paper, a chief must be able to cultivate a close working relationship with the city administration, particularly the appointing authority.

A candidate's experience is important to appointing authorities. While a detective commander may impress the public and some elected officials, the most competitive police chief candidates will be those who have a well-rounded background with the bulk of their experience in patrol command assignments, combined with administrative support command assignments, such as personnel management, budgeting and planning.

While technical competence, leadership, and a reputation for hard work may be all that is required for promotion in your own law enforcement agency, there is nothing like a solid professional reputation to catch the eye of prospective employers. The book on each of us is made up not only of what we have accomplished, but who we know, what we have written, and how we are regarded by those outside the agency. It is important that you develop a reputation by writing, teaching, and participating in programs that will give you a good name in your professional circles.

Note: The title, "appointing authority" will be used almost exclusively when discussing the relationship between the police chief and his/her boss. In many instances, the police chief's immediate supervisor will be a city manager, a mayor, a county executive, a board of police commissioners or another authority. The term "appointing authority" is used to simplify the text.

Beginning Your Search

Before beginning a police chief job search, ask yourself the following questions, and answer them as honestly as possible.

• Do I have the right skills, training and experience to be a chief?

• Are my credentials sufficient?

• What level of job might I compete for?

• Do I know how to write a résumé?

• How well do I perform when interviewed?

• Do I know how to prepare for an interview?

• Do I have sufficient negotiating skills?

• What makes up a good compensation package?

• What are my salary requirements?

This book will provide some guidance and information to help you hone the skills necessary for a successful job search. The rest is up to you. As you begin your search, keep the following job hunting basics in mind.

1. Develop a realistic career plan.

2. Do not accept a police chief position unless you have the necessary survival instincts.

3. Search consultants may play a significant role in the process.

4. Only a well-written résumé will get you an interview.

5. You cannot interview well unless you prepare and practice.

6. Appearance and general image play a significant part in the interviewing phase.

7. Once you have been offered the job, you control the negotiations.

8. You will not get any more salary than you ask for.

9. All major conditions of your job should be put in writing.

10. Because chiefs serve an average tenure of less than five years, the job hunting process is a continual and lifelong process. Knowing when to leave one position is as important as knowing when to seek a new one.

Police chiefs play a unique and critical role in today's society because police are on the frontier of social change. The chief routinely deals with the enforcement of laws (some popular and some less popular), politics, greed, bureaucracy, incompetence, cowardice and the failure of good intentions. Occasionally, the result is that police chiefs find themselves "in transition" (the code words for being fired) and they do not know how to search for another job. We hope this book will lead the aspirant to his or her first job and help those who are chiefs to continue to serve successfully.

Chapter 1

2 | Managing Your Career

Career Planning

MANY ASPIRING and current police executives fail to plan their careers. Some successful chiefs have relied on good luck and good timing. But the police executive job market is tougher than ever. Gone are the days when good credentials alone would get you a job. Today, with the ever-increasing pool of qualified men and women who have achieved substantial success in the profession, good credentials do little more than initially qualify an applicant. Because of the scrutiny and selectivity now used by appointing authorities, achieving the best jobs requires a combination of the right background, excellent interpersonal skills, and interviewing and negotiating skills. Engaging in career planning can give you a boost over other candidates, but police executives often are not prepared for the next phase of their career. Police chiefs' thoughts about career advancement are frequently unclear and ambiguous. Rare is the police executive who has a concrete, thoughtful career plan.

Career planning requires that you first determine your objectives. Some desire to lead a large agency due to the complex range of issues and responsibilities they will encounter. Others are interested less in the department's size than in directing a certain type of department or working in a certain area of the country. Others revel in the challenge of handling a "turn-around" job by fixing a "broken" department. Some want to be the change agent. Some do not want to follow a popular and successful chief, because it will invite certain comparison, and may not be flattering to the new chief. In any case, planning requires that you identify your objectives and what kind of agency you want to lead.

Ask yourself the following questions to begin the career planning process:

1. Do you have a definite career plan?

2. Do you have an alternate career plan?

3. Do you have an up-to-date résumé?

4.   Have you taken advantage of opportunities within your own agency for career development?

5.   Is your formal education competitive in today's job market?

6.   Are you conversant in contemporary police-related issues?

7.   Have you become involved in police-related activities beyond the scope of your own department?

8.   As a potential chief executive, are you sensitive to the importance of appearance and demeanor?

It needs to be noted that career planning is not synonymous with actively entering the job market. Rather, career planning requires that you consider possible career advancement strategies, and determine your career objectives, so that you are prepared to make choices that will lead to the best career for you.

Despite the benefits of career planning, few police executives do it well. One reason for the lack of planning is the understandable complacency we all feel when we are content with the status quo. What is the point of investing time and energy in planning for contingencies we are certain will never happen?

Another reason is that appointing authorities (those who are happy with their chiefs) generally do not encourage their chiefs to engage in long-term career development. While it may not be uncommon for managers to support deserving police executives in their quest for specific jobs that represent further advancement, extended formal support is almost nonexistent. It is simply not the custom of managers to encourage dependable employees to seek new positions outside the city. Appointing authorities take a proprietary interest in their police chiefs, and rightfully so because of their prior investment in the professional growth of their department heads.

Another clear impediment to planning is the fear that if colleagues learn that you are contemplating career options, it might jeopardize your professional standing. Again, planning is not synonymous with sending out applications. Indeed, proper planning can only strengthen your career options within your current department, because it forces you to analyze your options.

A desire for job security may also stifle career planning. The police profession is turbulent by any standard. Events and incidents that are typically beyond a chief's control may dictate job tenure. After all, chiefs usually serve at the pleasure of the appointing authority, and it may not take much for a chief to end up unemployed. Thus, there is an understandable hesitancy to abandon a secure police executive post for the unknown. To some, the potential price of reaching for a new position is often prohibitive.

Police professionals also hesitate to leave the security of the current position because new working relationships are unknown and may prove to be problematic, the cost of living may be higher, there will be significant emotional upheaval, and there must be a substantial commitment of energy to make the change. While these conditions may all exist, they must be balanced against the potential for a rewarding career that provides an opportunity for you to make your mark on a community and police department, as well as the police profession as a whole.

Career atrophy can also occur because of the strong commitment most police professionals make to the agency they serve. There always seems to be a pending crisis, major program or critical endeavor, the positive outcome of which many police professionals believe is dependent on them alone. This exhibits an admirable trait of police executives—the desire to finish the job once started. Appointing authorities find significant accomplishments to be compelling attributes in a job applicant. However, one mark of the truly successful leader is the ability to delegate and groom subordinates to continue key projects even if the leader moves on.

The Benefits of a Career Plan

A search may be stressful and disillusioning for candidates who do not engage in deliberate planning while they are happily employed. The time to plan and prepare is when life is good and there is ample time to think about your career objectives, not when the pressure of unemployment is upon you.

Without career planning, the best you can expect is a break-even situation, as described in the Lewis Carroll children's classic *Through the Looking-Glass and What Alice Found There:*

Alice, in answer to the Red Queen's question, states:

> "Well, in *our* country. . .you'd generally get to somewhere else—if you ran very fast for a long time as we've been doing."

The Queen's remark to Alice is worth our reflection:

"A slow sort of country!. . .Now, *here,* you see, it takes all
the running *you* can do, to keep in the same place. If you
want to get somewhere else, you must run at least twice
as fast as that!"

At the executive level of police management, there is little tolerance
for lack of career accomplishments. You must develop a career plan, work
at its implementation and be willing to take some chances if you want to
advance professionally.

For the most part, the people who have the best jobs in police chief
circles have operated with a career plan. It may not have worked exactly
as they originally intended, but it provided a basic blueprint to follow.
These police managers have made a series of strategic professional moves
resulting in career advancement. What these chiefs commonly possess
are energy and drive. Their prowess as managers does not dissipate over
the years but, rather, is invigorated by their career advancement. They are
looking, rather than waiting, for new challenges to satisfy their energies
and talents. If your objective is to climb the career ladder and find newer
challenges, then career planning is essential.

Different Career Paths Toward a Chief's Position

There are only about 500 agencies with appointed police chiefs serving
populations of more than 50,000 people. With more than 17,000 law enforcement agencies in the United States, most aspiring chiefs will work
at one time or another in a city of fewer than 50,000 residents.

Fortunately, the size of the city is not the measure of success. In fact,
the best jobs are not necessarily found in the biggest cities. Rather, your
ability to confront new challenges, cultivate organizational excellence,
obtain personal and professional growth, and achieve personal goals are
the real measures of success. The desire to be a police chief in a mid-sized
college town may require as much career planning as the hope to become
a chief in one of the nation's largest cities.

There are several common career patterns for police chief aspirants,
and they are determined for the most part by your rank when seeking a
chief's job, and the size of your department. Keep in mind that when an
appointing authority (or his/her designee) assesses you as a police chief
candidate, the most significant factor in that assessment will be your

present position. Second, your overall career progression will be a stronger factor than any one position (or assignment) that you held prior to your current one.

COMMANDERS IN SMALL AGENCIES

Supervisors or commanders in small departments of fewer than about 100 employees may be competitive applicants for smaller agency chief positions. Generally speaking, you need command-level experience before pursuing a chief's job. Supervisors in small agencies may also be candidates as smaller agency heads. Keep in mind that as departments diminish in size and there are fewer personnel to carry out agency functions, employees may assume a greater range of responsibilities. So a sergeant may have effectively served as a commander at times, and as a responding patrol officer at others. On the other hand, a smaller agency supervisor may supervise fewer officers than if he or she worked in a larger agency.

While there are many respected small departments, you may find greater opportunities with less well-known agencies. Some agencies may be characterized as troubled departments, but these situations, if carefully considered, can potentially be very rewarding. The opportunity to reform and revitalize an agency in distress can be very satisfying and can add great depth to your résumé. Some aspiring chiefs intentionally seek out agencies that need help and where one's talents can be appreciated. Think carefully before stepping into a chief's job on the heels of a highly respected chief. Expectations will be very high, and your inability to exceed them might prove detrimental to your career. In other words, it may not always be the best career move to pursue a situation with the very best department around.

The most helpful credential for police chief applicants is having been a police chief (ideally currently serving as a chief, rather than having previously retired or been out of the business for a few years). As a commander or supervisor in a small or mid-sized agency, your strategy could be to become a chief as soon as possible. This first chief's position might be considered a "hard duty" assignment because of the lack of job security, possible boredom, and the potential for a permanently damaged reputation. On the other hand, it has certain distinct advantages. By becoming a chief early in your career, you obtain experience as a chief executive, setting the tone for an agency, developing and managing a budget, and ideally, gaining stature and earning a reputation as a capable and competent police chief. You will gain valuable experience and visibility if other opportunities arise.

When securing your first chief's job, keep in mind what kind of agency you may want to pursue for your second or third chief's position. The appointing authority interviewing you for that second or third chief's job will put great weight on the experience accumulated during the previous job. So it needs to be as relevant as possible. Because you are accumulating a collection of experiences that improve your competitiveness, be selective about what opportunities you seize. For example, if you want to be competitive in municipal policing, then think carefully before taking a job in university or transit policing. These career moves are certainly not disqualifiers—they may even enhance your résumé—but you need to think beyond the current career move. Of course, some communities expect their chiefs to make a long-term commitment and not use a chief's situation simply as a stepping stone to something better. While personal and professional growth is critical, the aspiring chief needs to be respectful and understanding of community expectations.

CHIEFS OF SMALLER AGENCIES

It is common for police chiefs to advance from smaller agencies up to larger ones. The key is to determine how much larger an agency you should try for to still be considered competitive. A police chief often competes well for a department just more than twice the size of his or her current one. A smaller city police chief frequently has an edge when in competition with commanders from larger agencies. Having chief's experience, even in a smaller agency, will frequently give a candidate a better base of experience with which to compete.

COMMANDERS IN LARGER AGENCIES

Two basic patterns of career advancement exist for commanders in large, well-regarded police departments with more than about 100 employees. Differing pension systems and the rules for vesting largely dictate these patterns.

Commanders with the necessary experience, and the rank of captain, major or deputy chief (depending on the agency's rank structure) can realistically compete for the police chief position in a department with 50 to 100 employees. Frequently, these officers are in mid-career in their initial department, but are competitive for chief's jobs in smaller agencies. If their agency uses a "portable" pension plan so that they are fully or partially vested in the plan, this becomes a viable option. Others in agencies without any entitlement to any vesting rights may still choose to resign and take a chief's job.

More commonly, departments do not provide a "portable" pension, so commanders may remain in their initial agency until their right to pension benefits has been established, and then look for a chief's position. It is common for those at the top of the command structure in a large department—for example, a bureau commander, deputy chief, or even a captain—to retire and move into a police chief position. The principle disadvantage is that by staying in a command position for many years, you may pass by some promising opportunities to apply for a chief's position with another agency. The primary advantage of waiting is that you retain the security of retirement benefits, and gain extensive technical, supervisory, and administrative experience as a commander.

CHIEFS OF LARGER AGENCIES

Chief's positions in larger jurisdictions are limited in number. To be a competitive outside applicant for one of these top jobs requires having chief experience in a slightly smaller jurisdiction or having substantial second-in-command experience in a larger agency. It is worth noting that as the size of the jurisdiction increases, the pool of qualified police chief candidates for that agency diminishes. Conversely, the smaller the agency, the larger the pool of qualified applicants.

ADVANCING TO THE NEXT LEVEL

If you are a police chief with at least two-and-a-half years of experience and a record of accomplishment, you should be able to compete for positions as chief in other departments that are significantly larger than your present department. However, competing for jobs in departments more than three times the size of your current department is often too big a jump to realistically expect in one move. Do not set unrealistic expectations by repeatedly trying to compete when the odds are against you. Your career plan should be based on realistic goals in a competitive job market. There are, of course, exceptions to every rule and special circumstances where these common patterns will not apply. In other words, there are times when one will be competitive in spite of these general practices.

Developing Professional Experience and Knowledge

Developing a career plan involves determining the level of experience, education, training and knowledge that is necessary to achieve your career goals. Successful police chief applicants must take advantage of every opportunity for professional development and growth available to them within their departments as they progress through the ranks. These opportunities include rotating assignments, which allow you to gain balanced operational and administrative command experience; special assignments that provide unique opportunities for professional growth, such as managing a task force or accreditation process; public speaking assignments on behalf of the department or your division; or duties managing community outreach programs.

Education

To be competitive in today's job market, you not only need a track record of solid work experience, but educational credentials as well. The level of formal education among police administrators has dramatically increased in recent years. A 1975 survey, conducted by the International Association of Chiefs of Police (IACP) with support from the Law Enforcement Assistance Administration of the U.S. Department of Justice, indicated that slightly more than 14 percent of police chiefs had bachelor's degrees, and fewer than 5 percent possessed advanced degrees. By 1983, a survey conducted by the FBI and published by PERF revealed that about half of larger city chiefs had bachelor's degrees and 20 percent held advanced degrees. PERF's 1997 survey of 358 police chiefs in jurisdictions of more than 50,000 indicated that more than 87 percent had bachelor's degrees and 51 percent held advanced degrees, composed mostly of master's degrees with a sprinkling of law degrees and doctorates. The educational accomplishments of today's chiefs are even more pronounced for those chiefs who have been hired from outside an agency.

The most common route to obtaining academic credentials while employed in a police department is to attend a college or university part-time in or near your community. These programs, whether granting a bachelor's, master's or doctoral degree, will typically require several years of study. Additionally, there are nonresident degree programs now available through distance learning or computer-based curricula. Be certain that the institutions you choose are reputable, respected and appropriately accredited, especially if it is a nonresident program. Avoid institutions that advertise degrees by mail or award an excessive amount of credit for "life experience." If you are unsure about a school, obtain recommendations or references from alumni or faculty, your colleagues or the city human resources department.

When selecting an undergraduate major, do not feel compelled to choose a criminal justice field, such as police science or administration of justice. While a bachelor's degree in one of those areas may be helpful, other majors are fine, including English, history, education, mathematics or the natural sciences. On the other hand, graduate studies should focus on fields that will enhance your professional knowledge. Common choices are public administration, criminal justice, criminology, sociology, law, management or business administration.

Executive-Level Training

Attendance at executive-level training programs is another way to enhance your experience and education. The 1997 PERF study showed that 86 percent of the responding chiefs had attended some sort of executive development program, such as the FBI's National Academy, Law Enforcement Executive Development Seminar (LEEDS), or National Executive Institute (NEI); PERF's Senior Management Institute for Police; Southern Police Institute's Administrative Officers Course; Northwestern Traffic Institute's School of Staff and Command; Harvard University's Program for Senior Executives in State and Local Government; or similar programs. It is common for position announcements to suggest that the ideal candidate will have attended an executive development course.

Other Professional Activities

Take advantage of opportunities to get involved in professional police activities beyond the scope of your current job. These can include membership in regional or national professional associations that provide opportunities for committee work, publishing police-related articles, teaching or consulting. Becoming active on regional task forces can provide such opportunities. It is important to gain broad, first-hand experience in contemporary police issues beyond your own police agency. A number of national organizations are listed in Appendix C as sources of police chief job announcements, and are good associations to consider for professional membership.

Professional Reading

Building a career requires a commitment to understanding the business of policing. A prospective professional police chief must understand issues such as community and problem-oriented policing; the sociology of crime, victimization and offending; crime prevention through environmental design; and current developments in constitutional and criminal law. Chiefs must be familiar with and able to explain the evolution of contemporary police practices and thinking.

Competitive applicants will have read the leading texts in the field and be committed to remaining current on developments by reading professional journals and periodicals. Aspiring chiefs should invest in a personal library of the classics of police scholarship. An extensive reading list is included in Appendix H. Some familiarity with these texts and articles may come from formal study and education, but others will only be read if you take the time. At the same time, read the current periodical literature.

Knowledgeable chiefs should also keep track of publications distributed by the U.S. Department of Justice, including the National Institute of Justice, Bureau of Justice Assistance and Bureau of Justice Statistics. The National Criminal Justice Reference Service (NCJRS) can place you on a free mailing list to receive government mailings on criminal justice issues.

Grasping a larger understanding of the criminal justice field requires awareness of current literature in probation and parole, corrections and prosecution. Publications from relevant organizations, such as the National Criminal Justice Association, the National Association of District Attorneys, the American Correctional Association, the Academy of Criminal Justice Sciences (ACJS) and the American Society of Criminology (ASC) are just a few of the countless sources of information.

It is easy, of course, to remain isolated in the policing and criminal justice world and neglect other disciplines that relate to policing. For example, education, health care, civil law, urban planning, religion, economics, business, technology and community development are just some of the areas with a direct relationship to public safety and crime. A typical community's search committee for prospective chiefs will be composed of non-law enforcement people, such as educators, clergy, business people, lawyers and government officials. Your ability to make connections between your experience in policing and their experience can be very compelling, and it is only possible if you make a consistent effort to look beyond the police profession for ideas and knowledge.

Many communities also expect the chief to be aware of police-related events and trends occurring elsewhere in the country. Invariably, community members will hear, via television or magazine stories, about high-profile incidents involving other police departments, and you may be expected to comment on them. For example, the question could be whether the local police are prepared to deal with a similar set of circumstances. Make it a point to stay well informed. PERF's 1997 survey found that more than 85 percent of the responding chiefs regularly watch national television news, and a nearly comparable number regularly read a national or regional daily newspaper.

Searching for a Job

A variety of organizations provide valuable sources of information regarding available police executive positions. In Appendix C, we have included a list of professional associations whose newsletters publish job opportunities, as well as various publishers of policing journals, which sometimes contain job announcements.

While many police chief openings are advertised in national publications, some cities are still somewhat parochial with respect to the state or region where they recruit and identify candidates. Smaller jurisdictions especially may not advertise nationally. If you are interested in tracking vacancies in a certain state, you might contact the appropriate state League of Cities and ask to be placed on the mailing list for the newsletters or publications that list job opportunities. See Appendix A for state contact information.

You might also subscribe to newsletters published by state and regional police chief associations (see Appendix B). While many jobs are formally and widely advertised, others are not. You can become aware of these jobs through informal networks by maintaining contacts with colleagues active in the region where you want to work. Active membership in organizations—national, regional or statewide—increases those contacts and your chance of becoming aware of certain opportunities. Professional associations sometimes become aware of opportunities before they are officially advertised.

Major city or regional newspapers can also be an important resource. If you are interested in a particular metropolitan area or location, subscribe to that area's newspaper. Regional and national web sites may also post classified ads (see Appendix C).

As important as it is to review the classified advertising, it is also extremely helpful to read the news stories related to local police activity. News coverage may provide an early indicator that positions might become available, and affords potential applicants the opportunity to become familiar with local police issues. It is critical in a job interview to demonstrate knowledge of community concerns. This kind of knowledge helps to overcome a primary hurdle for an outside candidate—the belief of many hiring authorities that an outsider will have a distinct disadvantage in understanding local issues, customs and key players.

The Chronicle of Higher Education lists many positions for colleges and universities, including positions such as director of campus police, public safety or security. *The Campus Law Enforcement Journal* is another source.

The International City/County Management Association (ICMA) publishes a newsletter called the *Job Opportunities Bulletin (JOBS)*, which lists many positions available in city management, including police chief positions.

Internet resources for career information abound. See Appendix C for a list of some of the most useful sites.

3 | Political Influences

L IKE IT OR NOT, there are many political forces that affect the police chief selection process. Search committees, city council members, the news media, labor unions, special interest groups and current political events facing the community can all exert pressure and ultimately influence the final selection.

Search Committees

Because appointing authorities are now expected to seek community input on important decisions, search committees are increasingly common in police chief selection. Search committee members are generally chosen by the appointing authority. A close look at who is chosen can illuminate the various political constituencies in a community. Search committee members are sometimes chosen to reflect certain political power bases. Others are chosen because the appointing authority trusts those individuals to advise the group on the appointing authority's interests. Although committee members sometimes come to the table with preconceived attitudes concerning their constituencies' interests, often the committee develops common attitudes about candidate selection. As they begin to work together, the group's initial individual attitudes can sometimes dissolve into a more cooperative spirit. Nevertheless, it is wise to look closely at the committee's composition and understand what their interests are regarding the police department.

Because search committees often conduct the initial screening of candidates, they wield tremendous influence in the early stages of the process. If an appointing authority gives up the right to do the initial paring down of candidates, then he or she has little or no say in who is ultimately given the most serious consideration. If the committee rejects a candidate early, it is highly unlikely that the candidate will be reconsidered later.

Search committees also bring the history, culture and values of the community to bear on the selection process. Committee members often compare their own history, culture and values with their perception of these qualities in the candidate's community. Different parts of the country have different attitudes toward policing, based on their unique history and culture. Through discussions with search committees, it becomes apparent how these attitudes play a role in determining how well a candidate is accepted. Some search committees favor candidates from their area, because they are comfortable with people who are perceived as understanding the region's culture. They may even limit the search to a defined local area. California cities, for example, seem to prefer in-state candidates (there are, of course, exceptions). In any case, where you are from can be a factor in a job search.

A committee's cultural preference can work in your favor as well as against you. Candidates may come from a part of the country that is stereotyped as having different cultural attitudes from the hiring communities. That candidate may be viewed with a built-in bias that can be either good or bad depending on the stereotype. The police department where a candidate has worked may also have a reputation, either positive or negative, that will bias the committee. Generally speaking, if your part of the country and/or your department reflect a favorable image, you are at an advantage. If your department has been involved in a high-profile incident that reflected poorly on the agency, you will be at a disadvantage. The perceptions of one community can often differ drastically from another. While a reputation for a certain style of policing may be negative in one community, it may be positive in another. As a candidate, it is in your best interest to learn as much as you can about the local culture, history and attitudes in the community where you are applying. Try to become aware of the general reputation that outsiders have of the area where you are from, and the department in which you work.

Once a candidate is selected through a process involving a search committee, each committee member has a vested interest in the chief's success. Consider committee members to be valuable resources for opening lines of communication. They will likely go to great lengths to assist you in setting up meetings and creating opportunities for you to develop relationships with different segments of the community.

Confidentiality of the Process

When a search committee is involved, many candidates fear their names will be leaked to the news media for political advantage. An unscrupulous committee member who favors an internal candidate may decide to leak names of external candidates to the news media in the hope that a backlash may occur against hiring an outsider. Although sanctions may be taken against the committee member, the damage to the candidates is done. As more individuals are involved in a selection process, it becomes nearly impossible to guarantee anonymity. Candidates who participate in these kinds of searches need to assume that knowledge of their interest in the position will become public at some point during the process. Therefore, it is nearly always the best policy to immediately notify your superiors of your interest in the position, so that bosses are not blindsided by a reporter's calls or a story in the local newspaper. The more people who know of your candidacy, the better the chances are of information being spread more widely than you would like.

In some states, it is very difficult to maintain confidentiality due to state law. For example, Florida's Sunshine Law requires that under some circumstances, documents related to government business, including an executive search, must be made available to the public. Texas and Ohio have similar laws. Some states require that meetings of government officials (at which a quorum is present), even when discussing personnel issues, be open to the public. Research this issue early in the process.

City Council

Frequently during the search for a new police chief there is a tug of war between the appointing authority and the city council. Council members often feel they should contribute to the selection process. A wise appointing authority will find a way to involve council members, while retaining ultimate authority to make the final selection. Some police chiefs are selected by the appointing authority only with concurrence of city council. In this situation, it makes particularly good sense for the appointing authority to get the council's input before risking the selection in a vote. The last thing an appointing authority wants is to have his or her choice for police chief turned down by a public vote of city council. And it goes without saying that it can be devastating for a prospective chief to suffer this form of public rejection. Once a candidate is invited for an interview, it is advisable to find out what input the council will have in the process, and whether the appointing authority's choice is subject to council approval.

News Media

The news media are almost always extremely interested in the selection of a new chief. State and city laws vary regarding their openness to the media concerning the hiring of city officials. In some states, such as Florida and Texas, open records and meetings laws, or "sunshine" laws, prohibit communities from protecting the names of candidates for public positions. In these states, once you have applied for a job as police chief, your name and selected background information can become public information. Know the laws and practices of the community before applying for a job with the expectation of confidentiality. Again, in most cases, candidates are best advised to keep their supervisors fully informed of their interest in any search process.

Once community members have been identified as being directly involved with the search process, the media will seek them out for updates on the process. Occasionally, people who are not experienced in dealing with the media (and even those who are) are tempted to divulge confidential information. Some cities will intentionally leak names to the media as a trial balloon to gauge community reaction. The media will uncover information about the candidates through other media sources, as well as by talking to candidates' coworkers, community members and members of the union. This can be risky for both the city and the candidates but, unfortunately, it happens.

When names of candidates are released prematurely to the media, there is a career risk for police chiefs and aspiring chiefs alike. A chief risks losing credibility and the loyalty of subordinates if it appears that he or she is dissatisfied in the current position and is planning to leave. The issue of command succession arises, which can be very distracting as various commanders position for the expected selection process to fill the upcoming vacancy. The chief also risks being regarded as a lame duck. A chief whose name is suddenly announced as looking for another job is likely to come under considerable pressure from several camps.

Even the careers of aspiring chiefs, especially in large agencies, can be seriously compromised when interest in an outside agency is viewed as a sign of institutional disloyalty. However, the public generally accepts that some police commanders in their city will move on to become chiefs elsewhere.

Additionally, a reporter finds it much easier to unearth controversy surrounding a police chief than surrounding a police commander. Commanders are rarely a media target concerning sensitive police department issues. Chiefs always are. When reporters run a name search in their news databases, they will likely find frequent "hits" on a chief's name, but not a commander's. Remember that when your name goes public in the community where you are applying for a job, there is a good chance that local reporters will call reporters in your community to share the news.

The news media are sometimes an informal but significant stakeholder in chief selection. If the media have focused a lot of attention on the police department or even played a role in the previous chief's demise, they may take a strong role in attempting to influence the selection. A strong editorial calling for an outside chief who will turn the department around, or advocating the need for an insider to continue organizational development programs of the previous chief, can play a pivotal role in the selection process.

Labor Unions

Police unions and associations, whether established by formal contract or not, have a vested interest in the selection. Candidates will do well to learn about the history behind the union, their general attitudes toward city government, the issues they are most concerned about and their relationships with the previous chief.

While it is unusual for a city to give union officials a formal say in the final selection, many cities recognize the need to have union involvement at the front end of the selection process. Many search committees, head hunters and other officials charged with the selection process will consult with union members to get their opinions on the current state of the department and other appropriate issues.

Special Interest Groups

Special interest groups, such as the chamber of commerce and NAACP, often have either a formal or informal role in the process. They can wield significant influence. Know who these groups are, who their representatives are, what their relationship has been with the police department and what is important to them.

Current Political Issues

Recent issues facing the community and police department always come into play when a community develops a profile of their next police leader. Recent incidents regarding excessive use of force, increases in gang and juvenile violence, or increases in a particular type of crime are likely to affect the kind of professional experience a community will expect from its new chief. If there has been controversy surrounding issues such as curfews, concealed weapons and off-duty employment, interview questions will likely reflect these concerns. Be prepared to offer well thought out positions based on the best available research.

The Rumor Mill

A police department's rumor mill is generally a healthy network, and it is usually working overtime during a chief selection process. So many agendas and motives come into play during this time that it is often difficult to sort out fact from fiction. Nonetheless, be sensitive to both the informal and formal lines of communication. The rumor that a process is a "done deal" for someone may only be in circulation to discourage others from applying.

Insider vs. Outsider

An insider may have the advantage in a department that has not experienced any recent major controversy. But if change is the focus of the search, an outsider may have the advantage. Many jurisdictions will conduct a national search while also considering internal candidates. Others will consider only insiders, and some will focus only on outsiders. A close look at recent community events, as well as whether recent chiefs were from inside or outside, can give clues about which way a jurisdiction may focus the search.

Whether you are an insider or an outsider, it is tough to follow a legend. Comparisons will always be made. As an aspiring chief, you may do more for your career by going to a "distressed" department, as very often just showing up and making basic changes will be favorably noticed. It is also difficult to be the "first" anything when selected as chief, such as the first outsider, the first woman, the first African American, and so forth. There may be unreasonable expectations, especially in the first few months. This is not reason to avoid being a "first," but at least be aware of the potential problems.

Race and Gender

A community's demographics and current issues regarding race relations can affect how candidates are viewed, as well as the final outcome. Communities are increasingly seeking diversity in the candidate pool to include minorities and women. All candidates need to be sensitive to difficult issues such as police/minority relations, affirmative action in hiring, and promoting open communication in the workforce. Be prepared to respond to questions about how you would deal with sensitive race or gender issues in the community.

Knowing the current issues in a community can help determine what candidate qualifications are important to the appointing authority. But remember, appointing authorities and search committees do not always do what they initially set out to do. Attitudes can change. Issues are sometimes perceived differently once a search committee spends time together. They often develop a group mentality toward a decision that will be the best overall outcome for the department and community. A good candidate can sometimes get a search committee to see past their race/gender/insider/outsider biases.

Advice to Internal Candidates

Inside candidates are often in the awkward position of presenting their qualifications to people who have known them for years. It can be a challenge to convey that, although you have been a loyal follower under the previous chief, you are also a good leader capable of running the department. You will more successfully convey your ability to lead if you can back it up with examples. Take every opportunity as a commander to engage in public speaking. Be involved in new projects. Get additional management training. Work with the public and other city management officials. Doing so will develop your reputation as an emerging leader in the department. You must also understand the political influences that have been mentioned previously in this chapter. Do not fall into the trap of only concerning yourself with issues that relate solely to your area of command. It is impossible to develop a reputation as a leader in the department overnight. Do not wait until the chief announces his or her retirement before you start to take advantage of leadership opportunities.

Good and Bad Politics

To work effectively within large or small paramilitary bureaucracies, senior police commanders must be adept at dealing with internal politics. Only on occasion are they exposed to the politics external to the department. Nothing prepares you for the political arena in which a police chief operates. The chief may be protected from politics by a strong city manager or mayor but, to be successful, a chief has to understand local politics and how they work. Yet a chief must also be sensitive and not get caught up as a player aligned with any one special interest group.

Before seeking a chief's position, ask yourself if you have the patience or tolerance to work in the political arena. Some of the very best police professionals have concluded that it is an adjustment that they cannot make, and they have self-selected themselves out of further consideration. These officers have determined that they can better serve the profession in other capacities. Because the political dimension of being a police chief is so integral to one's job and survival, not everyone is cut out for being or should be a police chief.

Before applying for any police chief position, it is absolutely imperative that you get a handle on the political situation. If the department is under the influence of external partisan politics, with a history of providing political advantage to the local power brokers, or if there is any indication of patronage within the police department, subtle or otherwise, then you may want to avoid the job. On the other hand, politics is a component of a democratic society, and elected leaders and appointed managers must accept the inevitable give and take that is part of public decision making. The prospective chief must understand the ground rules before accepting the job offer. For example, does the appointing authority expect to be involved in the appointment of commanders? Is there a policy of providing extra protection for certain neighborhoods that are considered politically friendly, at the expense of other neighborhoods? It is better to discover such political expectations before you accept the job.

"Wired" Searches

Unfortunately, some appointing authorities begin a police chief search process, when in fact the outcome has been predetermined. These appointing authorities may feel political pressure to conduct what appears to be an "open" search, rather than simply appoint the person of their choice. Candidates who unknowingly apply for these positions may not only be wasting their time, but could also damage their professional reputations.

To avoid being compromised in such a process, a candidate may recognize certain "clues" that indicate a wired process. Numerous areas have been highlighted in this chapter that could lead to suspicions that a process is not truly open. Looking closely at the political environment and reading between the lines of what is said during the process may indicate the appointing authority's true intentions. In such a situation, it may be wise to withdraw from the process before your name goes public.

Once a process is over, if you are not chosen, try to find out why and what influenced the final decision. It can help you the next time. Avoid adopting a "sour grapes" attitude, even if you feel it had to be a "done deal," or that you were passed over because of bias. Give the search committee and appointing authority credit for doing what they felt was the right thing and try to improve your own chances of coming out on top the next time.

Fifty-Seven Varieties of Bosses

I was a city manager at the age of 27 and my first police chief was a 25-year veteran who was almost 50. Later, with more than 25 years experience as a city manager, I was working with a chief in his mid-30s. I'm not sure which chief got the worst deal, but one thing is sure, my management style has changed radically and each of them had to adjust to me, not me to them.

—William Kirchhoff

Hiring a police chief places appointing authorities at great risk. They cannot afford to make a mistake in filling this position. One can usually recover from hiring an ineffective parks director, but one rarely crawls out from under the fallout of a mistake in judgment regarding police chief selection. Going into the selection process, everybody will have a different opinion. The rank and file may want an insider, each top commander believes he or she is the clear choice, the business community wants a "law and order" chief, and so on. The match is more than between the police chief and appointing authority. It is between the city council and the chief, the community and the chief, special interest groups and the chief, and the organization and the chief.

Recognizing the importance of their decision, veteran mayors and managers go to great lengths to not only select the right person, but also to protect their flanks. As a potential candidate, you can bet the search process will be expansive, the background investigation thorough and the interview process exhaustive. If you become a finalist or the person hired, you can also count on being the subject of media attention, the rumor mill and personal criticism. The professional cost of becoming involved in the selection process can in itself be career elevating or career ending.

To be successful, the police chief will have to be acceptable to the business and ethnic communities, social service agencies, the police department, religious leaders, politicians, neighborhood organizations, and a wide array of criminal justice system players. Quite often these groups will be in conflict with one another and the chief will liken his or her role to the proverbial juggling act. Invariably, trade-offs will occur as limited resources are allocated to one interest rather than another.

There is no place to hide an ineffective police chief. The position is in the constant glare of public scrutiny. If the chief cannot handle the job, the appointing authority cannot afford to keep the chief afloat.

Regardless of whether you work for a city manager or mayor, the experience will be substantially different than your experience of working for a police chief. City managers or mayors, good, bad, or neutral, will be radically different for two reasons—they have a political view of the world, and they are accountable to the entire community, not just the police department. The comfort level you experienced as a senior commander, working for the chief and devoted to the single task of providing police services, evaporates when you become a police chief. Successfully adapting to the dictates, demands and requirements of a non-police professional or a politician can be exasperating and difficult.

It is incontestable that the appointing authority is boss and he or she, not just the police chief, is expected by the community to deliver a certain level of policing. Nevertheless, you should not accept a police chief position without the non-negotiable independence of controlling the police department personnel system, unequivocal control over assignments and operational deployment, and sufficient resources to accomplish the stated mission. Without these, no chief, no matter how adaptable or personable, can succeed.

Your relationship with your boss is the single most important professional relationship influencing your success as a chief in that community. Consider that relationship carefully before accepting the job. Know as much as you can to be reasonably assured that you will find harmony with that person's management style, attitudes toward police management issues, agenda for the community and department, and expectations of a police chief. Try to find out what kind of relationships your boss had with previous chiefs. Also ask about his or her career ambitions and consider the length of time he or she may hold the current position. Learn what political influences are likely to determine who succeeds him or her.

When to Leave

The same political influences that affect the selection process and the chief's daily activities can also dictate the time to call it quits. If you wait too long, politics can make it difficult for you to find another job. The best time to leave a job as a police chief is when everything is going as well as can possibly be expected, when you have made a record of significant achievements, and when you and the department have a good reputation in the community. Do not wait too long for the political winds of change to blow. They usually do.

CHAPTER 3

4 Managing the Process: The Role of Executive Search Consultants

G OVERNMENTS ENTERING the search process have two general choices available. They may manage the process themselves, or seek assistance from executive search consultants, also called executive recruiters or head hunters. PERF's survey indicated that slightly more than half of selection processes for major agencies were managed by the jurisdictions' personnel or human resources departments, without outside assistance. But for processes that openly sought outside candidates, executive search firm involvement increased.

Whether the search is spearheaded by city administrators or a professional search firm, many of the same steps must be covered. First, a brief objective analysis of the police department and issues in the community is undertaken. Second, that work is translated into a list of ideal qualities for the new chief. Third, those qualities are in turn translated into a job announcement. Fourth, the position is advertised and prospective candidates actively recruited. Fifth, résumés are screened and a list of top candidates presented to the hiring authority. Sixth, a slate of finalists is drawn up based on the list of top candidates, and interviews are arranged. Seventh, interviews are held and other selection tools used, including a careful review of references and a full background investigation. Eighth, an offer is made. Ninth, negotiations are facilitated and a candidate accepts the job.

Why Hire Outside Consultants?

Over the past 30 years, larger cities with a reputation for progressive administration have increasingly hired professional consultants to recruit qualified municipal managers, including police chiefs. Appointing authorities take several factors into account when they decide to retain outside help. First, and perhaps most important, they feel that consultants may know the applicant pool better, and will recruit more successfully. Cities do not hire police chiefs every day, so they do not know all the available talent or where to go find it. For example, authorities in a midsized Southern city recently conducted a selection process internally, but decided in the final interview phase that they wanted to recruit additional candidates. They hired a search firm to conduct a national search and enlarge the pool of candidates. Second, running a nationwide search may strain the city personnel and human resources staff. Hiring outside help may reduce that burden.

Certainly, hiring a firm is not inexpensive, but cities can justify it by pointing to greater costs if the search were directed internally. Undoubtedly, some cities hire a firm to provide a professional dimension to the search process, and a perception of greater objectivity. Some believe that bringing in executive search consultants lends credibility to the process, and that the final selection will be met with greater approval.

Because you as a prospective job candidate might encounter executive search consultants, it is to your advantage to understand why the consultants are used and how they operate.

Executive Search Consultants

Executive search consultants have experience and professional contacts that often make them more familiar with the pool of candidates and their respective strengths and weaknesses. Executive search consultants seek out and attract the best qualified candidates.

There are relatively few search firms that regularly deal with police chief searches. Most handle a range of municipal government searches, such as for city managers, finance directors, public works directors, and fire chiefs, as well as police chiefs. Other firms, such as PERF and IACP, have staff dedicated solely to police executive search. Firms generally receive a fixed fee to assist with a search process, or they devise some other fee arrangement with the employing jurisdiction.

At one time, city managers resisted executive search consultants. Today, however, this resistance is dissipating, as search consultants now play an important role in recruiting highly skilled professionals for municipal positions.

Executive search consultants retained by appointing authorities are charged with bringing to the interview process perhaps five, six or seven of the best qualified candidates they can recruit. Their job is generally measured by how the client evaluates all of the final candidates. Appointing authorities expect all of the finalists to be highly skilled and experienced professionals who are fully capable of running the department. Ultimately, search consultants must produce high-quality candidates for their client cities, and may take considerable time to carefully screen résumés, check references, talk to key leaders in the field and otherwise search for the right fit between the city and the available applicant pool. Additionally, the consultant will devote considerable time and effort to ensure that the applicant pool is reflective of the community and diverse, with strongly qualified candidates irrespective of gender or race.

Applicants who believe that executive search consultants are not giving them a shot at a particular job have to ask themselves three questions: (1) Do I have both the experience and educational credentials set by the search consultant's client? (2) Do I fit the job profile in terms of personality and managerial style? (3) Do I have the professional background the client is looking for? In many instances, when you are not a final candidate, you either did not meet the job profile, or some of your peers may have had better credentials. In some cases, in fact, you may have had competitive credentials, but your application was not perceived as having the right "fit." Consider asking the search consultant for advice on improving your chances in future searches.

Open selection processes are exceedingly competitive and the chances of obtaining the job are relatively slim. Chief vacancies in departments with approximately 100 officers typically draw more than 100 applications. To compete several times and not get any of the jobs is common. PERF's 1997 survey showed that a significant number of chiefs hired from outside had applied for several jobs before landing their first chief's position. Indeed, most outside chiefs had applied anywhere from two to six times. More than 10 percent had applied seven times or more, and a handful applied more than 50 times. Perseverance pays off.

The Executive Search Process: Step by Step

Most executive search consultants follow a similar process. However, processes vary based on the wishes of the client municipality, and the consultant's past experiences.

Initially, the executive search consultant meets with the appointing authority to determine the specific expectations for the next police chief. The consultant attempts to define departmental issues and identify major goals to develop a profile of the ideal chief. It is common at this stage for consultants to meet with community representatives, elected officials, police department and city employees, and others to obtain additional information. The profile is a reflection of what the municipality wants in terms of academic credentials, professional qualifications and job experience. It is the benchmark against which all applicants are measured.

Once the appointing authority has approved the profile, the consultant begins the search phase. Advertisements for the position are placed in appropriate publications. The search may also include contacting professional associations that can assist in spreading the word. Advertising, focused nationally, regionally and locally, helps ensure that a broad range of candidates are aware of the position and have the opportunity to compete. These advertisements typically consist of notice that the position is open, the salary range, a brief description of the qualifications, the minimum requirements for submission of an application, and a closing date. Résumés can be collected and acknowledged by either the city or the search consultants, depending on the arrangements made between the city and the firm. (See Appendix C for a listing of advertising sources.)

Individuals known to the search consultant who meet the position qualifications are contacted directly. Referrals from knowledgeable municipal officials, government organizations, city managers and police chiefs are followed up, and candidates recruited based on these recommendations. In many instances, these individuals would not otherwise apply for the position. To a great extent, this is the distinct advantage of hiring search consultants—they actively seek out these top prospects, many of whom they know either personally or by reputation. The very best candidates for the job are frequently not looking for work; they are happily and successfully serving other cities. It is the executive search consultant's task, as the city's advocate, to reach out to potential candidates and encourage the best of them to apply.

The executive search consultant may also review the proposed compensation package and advise the appointing authority whether it is sufficient to attract and retain the type of chief he or she wants. If it is not, the executive search consultant will encourage the client to increase the compensation and benefits to be competitive.

The consultant, having visited the city and spoken with many of the stakeholders, should be prepared to provide information to the candidates. Serious potential applicants may want to know about the city; its characteristics, such as the condition of its schools and housing costs; its problems; the socioeconomic characteristics and demographics; the city's financial condition; the police department's strengths and weaknesses; the city council and the community's expectations; and the background of top staff. Candidates who apply for a job where an executive search firm is handling the search should take advantage of the opportunity to talk with the consultant directly. From that one source, candidates can obtain much of the information they need to make an informed decision about whether to pursue the job. The executive search consultant will have information that will be difficult to obtain from other sources, such as the appointing authority's background and management style.

After screening résumés and conducting exhaustive background searches, search consultants will typically recommend to the appointing authority approximately 10 candidates who they feel best meet the qualifications. Many are eliminated from continued consideration, not because they are unqualified, but because there may be better qualified applicants, or because they do not fit the particular recruitment profile. Usually the appointing authority will select five to seven candidates from this list for interviews. The search consultant may also provide the client with a backup list of other qualified candidates, and should be prepared to provide the client with a list of all applicants who applied for the position. In advance of the interviews, the consultant usually provides the appointing authority with a summary of each finalist. This summary often includes a biographical overview along with reference checks and results of an online periodical check for the candidate's name. This profile gives the appointing authority a substantial amount of information about each candidate's managerial style, accomplishments and track record.

Once the finalists have been selected, the search consultant may be responsible for the substantive aspects of the interviews and any other screening mechanisms used, such as an assessment center. Both the applicant and the client benefit from this process. The applicants usually have an opportunity to obtain information about the community, take a tour of the community, and participate in a professionally conducted interview. The consultant wants to ensure that the candidates are well informed about the position requirements, and the community's conditions and issues, as well as the mechanics of the interview process. Typically the city pays candidates' travel costs to the interview, and arrangements for lodging, travel and scheduling are coordinated jointly by the city staff and the consultant.

Once the interviews have been completed and the appointing authority selects the top candidate, the executive search consultant often plays an important role in facilitating the employment negotiations and helping the parties reach a fair and equitable agreement. Before the final offer and acceptance, the consultant often arranges for a full background investigation. The investigation report ensures that the appointing authority is fully briefed on all aspects of the candidate's background. The negotiation step of the process has become more and more complex. The consultant is often able to suggest creative ways to resolve sensitive and complex issues, such as housing relocation expenses, employment agreements, house hunting trips, and alternative pension options. The consultant may advise the appointing authority on different ways that other municipalities handled these issues. The consultant may tell the applicant what the compensation parameters are and whether or not there is any room for negotiating. In short, the consultant is there to help find consensus.

Advantages to the Candidate

When a city uses a highly qualified executive search consultant, candidates generally benefit for a number of reasons. The consultant has a responsibility to assist all applicants and potential applicants during all stages of the recruitment process.

First, because the search consultant has visited and researched the city and its police department, applicants receive consolidated, relevant information about the position. Second, the applicant learns what the compensation parameters are and whether there is any room for negotiation. Third, the search process is accelerated and handled in an objective and systematic manner. Fourth, there is greater communication with the applicants and they are generally kept better informed.

And, finally, the executive search consultant can play a critical role as a facilitator and resource person during negotiations. They serve the city by focusing on candidates' particular concerns and providing the employer with information. As the intermediary, they serve applicants by understanding the appointing authorities' specific concerns, and how far they are willing to go to resolve them. The search consultant becomes a conduit for the exchange of information between the parties. Helping both parties reach consensus is as important as anything else they do in the process.

The Executive Search Consultant as a Career Resource

Executive search consultants are now a fact of life in the police chief job market. These consultants have played an important role in helping coordinate very complicated processes, as well as seeking out candidates who might not normally have applied for open positions. In many cases, the consultant is an invaluable ally of the city in encouraging ambivalent but superbly qualified candidates to consider a new position.

Police chief candidates, particularly those who are inexperienced, often fail to use the executive search consultant as a career resource. The currency of the police executive search consultant is the stable of well qualified and broadly experienced police executives whom the consult-ant has come to know by professional reputation and accomplishment. Consultants are always on the lookout for talent; that is what they get paid to do. You are encouraged to send them your résumé, and give them a personal call, even if you are not in the active job market. If you have the right credentials, as well as the right stuff, they want to know you. Find-ing qualified, talented police executives who are willing to relocate for the right opportunity is no longer an easy task. If you are thinking about a career move, let them know.

Most executive search consultants are more than willing to give career advice, and given their role, their advice is often very good. Answers to questions regarding career options and potential compensation, career preparation, and image and appearance are invaluable to a person formu-lating a career plan. When dealing with search consultants, first, advise them of your general career objectives. Second, let them know when you are interested in a specific position. Third, review the kind of position you are interested in directly with the search consultant. Finally, if a search consultant is handling a process on behalf of a city, all contact should be made through the consultant. It is generally not advisable to "end-run" the process because you have contacts in the recruiting city.

Some of the search consulting firms that are frequently involved with police chief selections are listed in Appendix D.

CHAPTER 4

5 | The Résumé

WHEN APPLYING for a position, remember that you are engaged in a competition. To be successful, you must package and present your work experience and professional achievements in a way that is impressive and compelling. Résumé submission is typically the first critical step in the selection process, and the first opportunity to present your qualifications. Your résumé and the manner in which it presents your experience and qualifications will most likely be the leading, and perhaps only factor that determines if you move on to the next stage in the hiring process.

A résumé serves another important purpose. It forces the writer to closely examine his or her career goals and determine what experiences and accomplishments are the most relevant. "The value of the résumé is not when it gets delivered, but when it gets created," said Yana Parker, author of the *Damn Good Résumé Guide,* as quoted in the Wall Street Journal (February 3, 1998, p. B1). "When people write their résumé, they really have to look at what's relevant to where they want to go." So a résumé is much more than a list of former positions and schools attended.

There is obviously more than one way to prepare an effective résumé. The following suggestions are designed to highlight your strengths and maximize the chances that your résumé is noticed and put on top of the pile.

Importance of the Résumé

For those reviewing applications, the résumé provides an opportunity to compare one applicant with others. There may or may not be specific recruiting criteria or an established system for screening or ranking résumés. Those reviewing them may be knowledgeable about the position in question, or they may only have a general understanding of the responsibilities. They may have little experience reviewing résumés in the police field, and may have no role in the ultimate hiring decision. One thing is clear, however; there will be people who are either impressed or unimpressed by the way your credentials are packaged.

From your standpoint, the résumé is, of course, the primary written vehicle for communicating your experience, accomplishments and overall qualifications. It permits the employer to initially compare you with other applicants, and it gives you an opportunity to separate yourself from the competition. It dictates the first impression others have of you.

Whether it is right or wrong, fair or unfair, those reviewing your résumé will draw initial conclusions about you. Their impression may be initially more influenced by the *appearance* and *organization* of the résumé than by the details of your *experience*.

Key Elements

A résumé will never substitute for a personal interview, but will determine whether you are given further consideration for an interview. A résumé should do two things: it should create a favorable first impression, and it should convey specific information about your background and experience.

The résumé's appearance is very important. At a glance, it will suggest whether or not you are organized and conduct your affairs in a businesslike fashion. The content is also important. It can send messages about your leadership abilities, and whether you are knowledgeable of current police practices and innovative in your thinking. It will suggest whether your experience has been broad or limited, and whether you have accumulated significant achievements. It provides clues about your management and supervisory capabilities, and insights into your personality. It can signal your level of interest in the particular position under consideration, and whether you have the appropriate background and record of accomplishment to succeed in it.

The résumé should convey specific information about your work history and educational background. The résumé must present a clear outline of the responsibilities you have routinely shouldered. It must highlight the level of the tasks you are capable of handling, and any outstanding or unusual strengths. While there are obviously limitations on length, the résumé must provide the person reviewing it reasons for giving you further consideration as opposed to others.

A good track record will speak for itself, but the résumé must communicate it. If it fails to do so, it will eliminate you from further consideration.

Initial Research

It is not necessary to prepare a new résumé every time you apply for a position. However, in combination with the cover or transmittal letter, the package must be customized for each position sought.

To create a favorable first impression, use the cover letter to make obvious your interest in the position. If you convey some specific knowledge of the community and what it desires from its next police chief, you will have separated yourself from other applicants. No one will expect you to know everything about a new community, or even about the position itself, but a general understanding of the community and its challenges can be helpful. (This knowledge may also help you decide not to apply.) Each situation is different, and you must obviously use good judgment in how you conduct your research. The goal is to gain information about the community, the scope of the job, particular issues that must be dealt with, and special or unique objectives that must be met.

If an executive recruitment firm is involved, it can be an excellent resource. While the firm is retained by the employer, they also have a responsibility to attract and encourage potential candidates. The firm can tell you about the community and what the city is looking for in the successful applicant. Establishing rapport with the firm at the beginning of the recruitment process gives you an opportunity to distinguish yourself from the competition. More important, the information the firm supplies you about the community and the position will help you in customizing a résumé and cover letter.

Preparing the Résumé

There is no rigid rule governing how long or short a résumé should be, but it must be long enough to be reasonably complete, and short enough to be read briefly. A one-page résumé is generally too short, and a 10-page résumé is too long. Shoot for no more than about three pages. This length also forces you to identify and select career experiences that are most relevant. Some applicants prepare a summary-type résumé and a second expanded résumé with career details. Unless there are some extenuating circumstances, a single résumé is preferable.

In organizing the résumé, anticipate questions that a prospective employer is likely to pose, and make your résumé responsive.

Police executives should follow a chronological format rather than a functional format. A functional résumé is organized around themes of skills and abilities, while a more traditional chronological résumé outlines a career progression over time. Because police organizations are paramilitary structures, career progressions for police professionals are relatively similar. A chronological summary of your career is a more effective way to compare your experience with your competitors'. On the other hand, if you have limited work experience, you may choose a functional format to emphasize that you possess the requisite skills and abilities, but have not had the depth of occupational experience.

Even if a chronological model is most appropriate, however, it is a good idea to write a functional résumé as an exercise. We tend to define ourselves linearly and chronologically, and failing to reflect on the sum of our experiences. Preparing a functional résumé may force you to summarize the key skills and abilities that qualify you for the job, and will help prepare you for an interview or oral board.

Basic Information

A résumé must contain your name, address, and home and work phone numbers. A home phone number allows recruiters or the appointing authority to contact you on the weekend or in the evening. Include an e-mail address if you have one.

The Critical Areas

The following are the four most critical areas to highlight on your résumé:

1. What is your current position? (Include the name of your agency, your rank and your current assignment.) What have been your major accomplishments in this position?

2. How long have you held your current position?

3. How has your career progressed to this point? What were your previous assignments, ranks and agencies, if different from your current one?

4. What is your highest level of education? (Include type of degree, name of institution, date degree was received, and any honors awarded.)

When you consider the format of your résumé, these four points should be easy for the reader to distinguish. Use spacing, headings, margins, font size, and bold type to clearly communicate these points. It has been estimated that during the initial screening, the reader reviews each résumé for less than one minute. Whether that quick impression is positive depends on how well you communicate these four critical points. After this initial screening, the reader will review the favorable résumés in more detail.

Education

Information about your undergraduate and graduate education is an essential component of any résumé. Include the name of the school from which you received your degree, its location, the major or principal course of study, the type of degree earned, and the month and year it was received. Be sure to list formal schooling even if no degree was received. Your education should be listed in reverse chronological order, with your highest degree listed first. If you have an advanced degree, such as a master's or doctorate, list your education before your work experience. If you do not, list your work experience before education.

Although it is not necessary to list where you attended high school, there may be reason to include it. For example, you may want to show your connection to and familiarity with a certain geographic area. Information about your grade point average is not essential, but academic honors such as membership in Phi Beta Kappa, or significant scholarships or fellowships, will often catch the reader's eye. Course work after college should be selectively noted. It is helpful to show some commitment to continuing education. Be hesitant to list routine police training courses or certifications. For example, in-service training in defensive tactics, firearms or DUI/DWI enforcement is not suitable for inclusion in the résumé.

Include your participation in nationally recognized management-level training: the FBI's National Academy, LEEDS and NEI; the Police Executive Research Forum's Senior Management Institute for Police; Southern Police Institute's Administrative Officers Course; and Northwestern Traffic Institute's School of Staff and Command are a few leading examples.

Work Experience

Because prior experience is the best indicator of future success, this is the most important part of the résumé. Ensure that it is described in sufficient detail so that your experience, responsibilities and accomplishments are clear. Information should be in reverse chronological order, with your current position listed first. Be selective in listing jobs held prior to your law enforcement career, or that are completely unrelated to criminal justice, especially positions held during high school or college, or part-time jobs. If they truly strengthen the résumé, you might consider including them. However, leave out jobs that occurred early in your career and that do not contribute to your professional qualifications. Internships or similar experiences that have a relationship to your career should be noted briefly.

Preceding each job description, give a brief overview of the organization where you worked. If you have worked for more than one organization, do this for each one. Briefly describe the community that you served, listing city and state, population, demographics, size, type of community, etc. If your community is a capital city, has a university, is part of a major metropolitan area, has been growing rapidly, has a diverse population, or is a resort community, you should say so in your description. Then briefly describe the police department, listing the size of the staff, the budget, the type of policing strategies utilized, major departmental accomplishments such as accreditation, whether the department has collective bargaining, etc. This allows the reader to identify with the environment where you have worked. If possible, mention factors that are similar to the organization where you are applying, or areas in which the organization might want to be similar to yours.

Focus on your principal responsibilities and accomplishments. Try to highlight the variety of experiences you have had. Do not include a narrative from a job description. Do not talk in abstract terms about your career experiences. Be specific, and relate what you have accomplished in each command-level position. Include the following kinds of information for current and previous positions.

1. **Title of position:** List your rank and assignment.

2. **Name of the employer and dates of employment:** Include a brief description of agency and community, as discussed above. Indicate the dates of employment for each position with month and year.

3. **Data regarding your area of responsibility:** Include services provided, number of employees supervised, and budget.

4. **Scope of responsibility:** Keep this brief. Identify the area of the organization for which you were responsible. If your responsibilities included dealing with labor-man-

agement issues, indicate that here. Emphasize areas of responsibility that are similar to those of the position for which you are applying.

5. **Accomplishments:** How well you describe your accomplishments may be the single factor that puts you ahead of other candidates. List major achievements for each command-level position that you have held. Include special projects or assignments, changes that you made in the delivery of services or the operation of your given unit, community outreach activities, and any other special activities that resulted in improving the overall operation of your organization. For example, make very clear your involvement in community policing or problem-solving initiatives, and community outreach in diverse neighborhoods.

Information about current and past work experience has to be complete without being burdensome. The descriptions of your most recent positions and accomplishments should be the most detailed, because they are most relevant to the position for which you are applying. You should generally write less about each position as you go backward in your chronology of work assignments. It is not necessary to describe in detail your supervisory and nonsupervisory assignments prior to command-level experience. A general summary of these assignments is sufficient. For each command-level position, or positions with a high degree of latitude or authority, describe what you accomplished.

Professional Activities

This portion of the résumé allows readers to judge your leadership and accomplishments in the policing profession, outside of your agency. Express your commitment to the police profession by indicating your involvement in professional activities that go beyond the scope of your specific job.

Include membership in related professional organizations, articles and publications you have authored, programs you have taught, and committee work. Do not list every speech you have given, every conference you have attended, every course you have taught, and every certificate you have received. Rather, be selective and provide a good overview of all achievements. List only the most important activities, and be specific by indicating the nature of the activities, offices held, and the honors received. In a word, this section should show that you have a commitment to the profession. A listing of many memberships will not distinguish you from others, and is not as helpful as indicating active participation in a few select organizations.

In addition, consulting experience may be listed here. However, it should not appear that your consulting experience has interfered with your primary employment. Involvement in community service and charitable organizations may also be included, but be wary of indicating involvement with social, political or religious organizations.

Military Experience

List your dates and branch of service. Include any duties or awards directly relevant to your professional development or leadership experience, especially any time spent in command positions.

Personal Information

Employers are legally prohibited from asking certain personal questions of job applicants, nor can they base any employment decisions on these factors. But that does not mean prospective employers are not interested; some like to know personal characteristics such as your marital status, number of children and date of birth. Although it is not necessary, if you do not mind sharing this information, you may include it. Do not list hobbies or your health status on your résumé.

General Résumé Guidelines

It should go without saying that you should never make misleading statements on your résumé. Use proper grammar and punctuation, and spell all words correctly. Never use acronyms or abbreviations. Listing a job or career objective at the beginning of your résumé is unnecessary. It should be clear in your cover letter that your objective is to get the job for which you have applied. Keep sentences short. Although the cover letter should be dated, do not include a date on your résumé. Do not send the résumé in a folder or with a cover.

For emphasis, use bold type rather than underlining or italics, except when using italics for book titles and names of magazines or journals. Article titles should be in quotes. A general rule is to use serif fonts (e.g., Times Roman, Palatino, Garamond) for text, and sans serif fonts (e.g., Helvetica, Arial, Universe) for headings. Use no more than two fonts on your résumé. Use bold and/or enlarged font size for headings. Font sizes should generally be between 10 and 14 points. If you are trying to condense the length of your résumé, you may reduce the type to 10 points; however, some may find that difficult to read, and it may not transmit well by fax. Twelve-point type is easiest to read. Never update your résumé by hand or in a different typeface.

Printing

Although a résumé need not be professionally printed, it must be neat and businesslike. Résumés and cover letters should be printed on plain good-quality paper. A candidate should never use police agency letterhead for a cover letter inquiring about a job. The too-common practice of using official stationery raises serious ethical questions and may lead some appointing authorities and consultants to heavily discount your potential. Never send a photocopy of your résumé. Do not use a professional résumé writing service.

References

Your résumé should include an attachment of at least three and no more than eight current work-related references. Work-related means that they have some ability to comment on your skills as a leader and manager. Ideally, they should include your current and most immediate supervisor, as well as other supervisors with whom you have worked. In some cases, a desire to keep a job application confidential may prohibit inclusion of a supervisor. In addition to supervisors, your list may include colleagues and associates. Those you know professionally are the most effective references. For example, include council members, union presidents, community leaders, neighboring police chiefs, city attorneys, and personnel directors. Avoid listing subordinates and those with whom you have solely a personal relationship, such as a neighbor or family minister. Avoid listing a reference solely because he or she holds a prestigious position, such as a congressman or judge.

Your list should be diverse and include people who have knowledge of your qualifications as a police manager, both inside the department and in the community. Your references should all be able to speak to your *current* qualifications; do not limit your list to supervisors from five or 10 years earlier. It can be helpful to include individuals who have significant police management experience. Be sure to obtain their permission each time you use them. List their full names and their titles as they relate to your job. Include their full address and a work phone number. Ask permission to use their home telephone number as well. Provide them with a copy of your résumé and explain to them how they can best help you. It may be appropriate to ask the reference what he or she would say about you.

If you have dealt with controversy that may cause concern about your qualifications, choose references who are knowledgeable about the issues. Ask your references to deal with the issues directly and candidly if contacted by a potential employer.

You may want to change your list of references depending on the position for which you are applying. For example, if you know someone who would serve as a reference, and who is somehow connected to the city in which you are applying, use him or her. The likelihood that the person assessing your résumé will pick up the phone and call a reference if they see a familiar name is very good. The endorsement of a trusted colleague can be the most powerful tool in getting you from the résumé stage to the interview stage.

Be aware that by providing references, it is very possible that the word may soon circulate in your hometown and department that you are a candidate for another job. If you would like to be notified before your references are contacted, indicate so in your cover letter.

Attachments

Other than references and a cover letter, attachments to the résumé are generally not recommended. However, there may be occasions when you may want to attach a recent favorable editorial or feature story highlighting your accomplishments or those of your department. Be careful, however, that you do not cross the line and appear to overpromote yourself. Submitting your photograph is not recommended, although if it appears in the context of a newspaper article, it might be appropriate. You may attach a copy of your department's annual report if you feel that it would be helpful in describing your department and your accomplishments.

Unless they are requested, do not send letters of reference, college transcripts, training certificates, performance evaluations, or military discharge papers with your résumé.

Preparing the Cover or Transmittal Letter

Many applicants overlook the importance of a cover letter. Some view this exercise as pro forma, and miss a valuable opportunity to distinguish themselves. Cover letters should be specific to the city that the applicant is applying to, and incorporate information that will capture the reader's attention. The letter's purpose is to express interest in the position and briefly relate your past work experience and accomplishments. The cover letter ought to make you and your previous experience stand out, and indicate why you believe your background and accomplishments would be a good fit for the city. If it does, you will have an advantage over the competition.

While your résumé summarizes your career and credentials, the cover letter focuses on the specific position and city for which you are applying. If there are gaps in your work history, briefly explain them in the cover letter. Do not list your education and experience compared with the education and experience listed in the job announcement. This gives your letter a challenging tone.

Cover letters should be original, not photocopied. Like résumés, they should never be handwritten or on agency letterhead. Consider investing in personal business stationery or set up your printer so that your name and address appear professionally printed at the top of the letter. The letter should be concise and not exceed one-and-a-half pages.

If you are responding to an advertised vacancy that requests salary information, it should be presented at the end of your cover letter.

The following is a sample outline for a cover letter:

Opening paragraph: Make a direct statement about why you are writing, why you are interested in the position, and how you heard about the vacancy.

Second paragraph: Tell the reader what you currently do. Explain why your background is particularly appropriate for this position. Highlight your career accomplishments and qualifications.

Third paragraph: Give a summery of your formal education. Emphasize how your education fits this position.

Fourth paragraph: Use this paragraph to sell yourself. Describe what makes you different from, and better qualified than other applicants.

Closing paragraph: Show an interest in coming for an interview at the reader's convenience. Make it easy for the reader to contact you by giving your phone number. Provide salary history information, if it was requested in the job announcement. Indicate whether you would like your candidacy to be kept confidential.

Review and Edit

Once you have drafted your résumé and cover letter and decided on attachments (if any), always have others review your drafts. It is vital to eliminate any spelling or grammatical errors. Search committee members view spelling mistakes and grammatical errors as symptomatic of professional carelessness. Police chiefs must convey thoughts effectively in writing, and this is the first opportunity to make a solid impression on the reader. Get the opinions not only of your peers in policing, but of others who have the same background or perspectives as potential search committee members. Do not be afraid to call on professionals in the field to review your résumé and cover letter and provide you with feedback.

Appendix E includes sample cover letters, and Appendix F contains sample résumés.

6 | Interviews, Assessment Centers and Other Screening Methods

Speaking without thinking is like shooting without aiming.
—W.G. Benham

Interviews

WHY PREPARE FOR AN INTERVIEW?

A well-written résumé can increase the chances that you will receive an interview either from a recruiter or from the appointing authority. It is, however, a good interview resulting from thorough preparation that creates a positive chemistry between an interviewer and interviewee, and moves you to the next stage in the hiring process. Once the interview begins, the chemistry that is created (or not created) in the interview transcends the written résumé. You can no longer rely on your credentials alone. A candidate with lesser qualifications who interviews well is likely to take the lead over a candidate with better qualifications who interviews poorly. It is rare that one can overcome a poor interview.

Do not become overconfident if invited for an interview. You clearly have the necessary credentials to proceed to the next stage in the process, and your chances have improved considerably from when you first applied. However, you are now in head-to-head competition with at least four to six other professionals with comparable experience and track records. If all other things are equal, the chances of being offered the job are now perhaps one out of five, or 20 percent. To better your odds, prepare for the interview.

The time you spend in an interview is one of the most important events in your professional life. Where you live, how much you earn, and where your children are raised and educated are frequently determined by how well you perform in an interview. Despite its importance, most people never practice being interviewed, or think through how they are going to answer difficult questions, or even the most basic ones, such as, "Why do you want this job?" Preparing for an interview will help you decide if you want to remain a candidate for the job. And it will no doubt impress the interviewer that you have done your homework.

If during your preparation you learn that this is not the job you want, then you should drop out of the process right away. It may hurt your chances of being seriously considered in future processes if you go through the motions just for the experience, and end up being offered the job only to decline it. City managers and mayors talk to each other, as do personnel directors and executive recruiters. You do not want to gain a reputation as someone who is just testing the waters.

HOW DO YOU PREPARE?

There are five steps to interview preparation. First, review whatever reports and printed information are available from the organization with which you will be interviewing. Second, make personal contacts with people who may know something about the job. Third, visit the community before the interview. Fourth, enhance your conversational and public speaking skills by gaining teaching experience and giving informative presentations. Finally, and perhaps most important, thoroughly assess your strengths and weaknesses as well as the "image" that you present. Executive search consultants generally agree that, as superficial as it may seem, the image you project at the initial interview is a key determinant of whether a job offer will be forthcoming. Because of its importance, a chapter in this book is devoted to this subject.

INFORMATION REVIEW

It is fairly easy to gather a significant amount of material on the community and police department. A good place to start is the city's web site, if there is one. Do not hesitate to request information directly from the city. Learn as much as possible about the city's financial condition. The last thing a prospective chief wants to do is to take a job without a complete understanding of the city's financial realities. Request copies of the city's budget and audit, as well as the police department's annual report and budget. If applicable, request a copy of the department's labor agreement(s). If asked to participate in a second interview, you may request more detailed information, such as the department's policies and procedures, and the city's personnel rules.

Verify who makes the decision on hiring a police chief and to whom the chief reports. Most often the police chief is selected by and reports to either a city manager or mayor. However, some communities vary from this structure based on their city charters. For example, there may be a police and fire commission that actually hires the chief, although the chief may report to the city manager, who has no say in the selection. Often, a manager or mayor can make the decision, but it must be confirmed by the city council. It is beneficial to know how the process works and what everyone's concerns are.

The chamber of commerce in most cities can provide a wealth of information about the community. This is a good place to find out about local points of interest, recreational and cultural activities, business and development issues, city demographics, housing information, etc. You can also request information from the school board if you have school-age children. At a minimum, you should know some basic facts about the community, including geographic features, population size and demographics, major highways, and its proximity to major cities and airports. During the interview, convey your general knowledge of the community. Interview committees often distinguish between the candidates who have learned something about the area, and those who have little knowledge of the community and appear to be simply job hunting.

Research why the last police chief left and what critical issues are facing the police department and community. Try to find out a little bit about the department's history, such as how many chiefs it has had in recent years, the reasons for their departures, and if they have had any major lawsuits, court orders, labor disputes or scandals. It is also helpful to find out something about the stability of city government, such as how many city managers there have been in recent years and the turnover rate of city department heads. Much of this information can now be accessed on the Internet from local newspapers' web sites and in their archives. To really understand a community, subscribe to the local paper during the selection process. Before the interview, be sure you are aware of any current issues that are attracting media coverage.

When reviewing the newspapers, you should do three things. First, read the issues published immediately before the announcement of the job vacancy. They may explain why the job is vacant and what caused the former police chief to leave. Second, read about the last election. Try to identify major issues of public concern. Find out when the next election is, and how long the mayor and council members have in their current terms. Try to determine the concerns of the appointing authority and what he or she is looking for in a chief. Third, read different editions of the newspaper, and be sure to check the sports, arts and real estate sections to develop an overall sense of the community.

A review of current and past issues of the FBI's Uniform Crime Reports (*Crime in the United States*) helps you get a feel for recent crime trends in that location. *The Municipal Year Book,* published annually by the International City/County Management Association, also contains excellent information on city statistics. If nothing else, this type of information helps you to develop a general community profile. The U.S. Census Bureau web site also provides important statistical information on every community in America.

Conduct research early and in depth. It will help you decide if you really want to be a candidate for the position. It is time consuming, but in the end it may save everyone a great deal of aggravation. It may be difficult to obtain some of this information, and you might have to put off doing much in-depth research until a visit. But, if possible, you are well served if you can develop a sense of the community and the police department before actually going to the interview.

PERSONAL CONTACTS

A candidate should also talk to any professional or personal contacts who may have information about a chief's vacancy. It is possible, if one knows the right people, to gain insight into the position from those who are often able to "read between the lines." However, continue looking at the media coverage, because that is what the public sees and very likely what influences and motivates the hiring authority. Personal contacts may supplement your knowledge, but do not neglect the basic sources. Furthermore, you can do yourself or your contacts a great deal of harm if you inadvertently raise confidential or controversial issues during the interview that have not been released publicly.

Other police chiefs or commanders in the area may have a better idea of what the true picture is than what is depicted in the media. A candidate may want to contact the police chiefs' association in the state for more information on a position. Be cautious using this resource because an association may advocate for local candidates. They may be especially helpful, however, if you have identified a specific state as a location where you would like to work. In any case, to understand the situation, and compete successfully, you must have information. Do not hesitate to ask questions.

COMMUNITY VISIT

If possible, arrive at least a day before the scheduled interview. You can only obtain a limited amount of information by reading reports and making phone calls. The best sources of information are in the community itself.

Once you arrive, rent a car and tour the community. Evaluate the place from two perspectives: will your family enjoy living there, and do you want to work there? You can learn a lot by driving through the residential and business districts. Look at the schools and pick up a recent real estate listing magazine. Follow up on what you learned from your reading and conversations. The value of homes, condition of public facilities, availability of shopping, and the location of parks and schools will help determine if you want to live in the community.

You will certainly want your spouse to accompany you on the second interview to look at potential living arrangements. However, you may want to consider bringing your spouse to the initial interview (at your expense). You will be glad you did if the appointing authority pressures you for a response to an offer, but declines to give you a follow-up interview to which you can bring your spouse.

While it is wise to drive by the police facilities, look at the condition of the fleet, and observe officers on patrol, it is not advisable to introduce yourself to officers or attempt to tour the building. These actions may only serve to fuel the rumor mill and provide you with biased and inaccurate information.

Try to get a "feel" for the community before you go into the interview. An experienced police executive should be able to pick up critical information before he or she is actually interviewed. The more you know when you get to the interview, the better off you are. Frequently the interviewer will ask you what you think about the community. The question is a lot easier to answer if you know something about the city and you can say something positive.

PUBLIC SPEAKING SKILLS

The better your public speaking skills, the better you present yourself in the interview. By gaining experience giving presentations, you enhance your ability to compete effectively in the interview. Take every opportunity to teach in your academy or local college, and to give presentations in front of community groups.

INTERVIEWING DEMEANOR

You want to present yourself as the ideal candidate for the job. You should appear confident, enthusiastic, mature and intelligent. Good body posture, eye contact, a strong handshake and clear articulation are necessary. Exude controlled confidence and energy. Respond directly to the questions and cut down on verbosity. Avoid small talk, trivia, clichés, and use of acronyms and common police jargon. Humor, if used properly, can help reduce the inevitable tension of the interview process. But this does not mean you should tell jokes—rather, be yourself and show a sense of humor. The best interviews are conversational in nature.

Do not assume a subordinate role during the interview. While politeness and respect should govern your behavior, remember that the appointing authority on the other side of the table wants to hire a leader. They want a "take charge" person. For example, it is inadvisable to address committee members as "sir," or "ma'am," because first, it puts you in a subordinate position, and second, it sounds overly formal. You are being interviewed because your performance record indicates that you have the skills and talents they need; now they want to hear what you have to say. This does not mean that you should be arrogant. It means that you should feel comfortably equal with the interviewers. You are not going to get the job if you appear unsure, passive or lacking in confidence.

Do not pass out material during your interview unless the interviewer asks for specific documents. Passing out annual reports, writing samples, biographical information, strategic plans and public relations materials during an interview can be distracting to the interviewer and take the focus away from you. If you have prepared by becoming knowledgeable about the target job and you effectively communicate your qualifications, you can be successful without props or handouts. Preparing an unsolicited "plan of action" that you would undertake as a new chief appears presumptuous. Only present materials in an interview if you are requested to do so.

It sounds overly simple, but be yourself. Trying to anticipate what the interviewer wants and then portraying yourself as something or someone you are not can only backfire. Even if they do not sense the inconsistency, if you are offered the job, you will eventually have to revert to your true self and both you and your employer will be unhappy. They will discover that they did not get who they thought they were hiring. It is not worth it.

Be aware of how your appearance, personal mannerisms and attitude affect your communication. Body language provides strong nonverbal messages to your audience. When a person gives off contradictory verbal and nonverbal messages, it is likely that the nonverbal ones will be believed. In other words, you may tell your audience that you are a confident leader, but if your body language does not support your words, your body language will have the greatest effect on your listeners. Studies have shown that the content of your presentation in an interview plays only a minor role in your total impact. Your tone of voice and the nonverbal elements, such as how you dress and body language, make up a large part of how you are evaluated. While many professionally competent applicants think that their experience and qualifications should get them the job, it is generally agreed that an interviewer's decision is based 50 percent on image, 45 percent on personal communication style and only 5 percent on substantive information conveyed.

This is not to say that experience is unimportant to the overall process. It is evaluated before you get to the interview and it plays a major role in whether you make it to the interview stage at all. It can also play a major role after the interview. But the interview itself allows the appointing authority to assess other factors such as your personality, attitude, confidence, humor, intelligence, enthusiasm, communication style, political savvy and judgment. In a sense, you have already been deemed to have the basic qualifications and right experience. The question now is whether there is the right "chemistry" between you and the appointing authority.

To take a critical look at your own interviewing skills, it can be helpful to set up a mock interview in front of a video camera. This can be extremely helpful in assessing body language, mannerisms and speech patterns that might detract from your overall presentation.

Take a long, hard look at who you are, what you do well (and not so well), and where you have succeeded and failed. Be prepared to draw parallels between your own situation or past experiences and the hiring community's. Give some thought to how others view you. If you cannot tell the interviewers what your current boss thinks of you, they might assume you are not very perceptive or self-aware. You should expect to be asked about your failings as well as strengths. Do not give meaningless or self-serving answers. Sincerity and self-awareness, even in the form of recognizing one's own faults, go much further in boosting your credibility.

You will almost always be asked why you are interested in this particular job. Be prepared to answer in a concise, specific, articulate way. Do not spout platitudes. Draw on your own experience, identify specific aspects of this position and community, and explain why they are complementary.

During the interview establish that you

- are forthright and honest,

- are a proven and capable leader,

- can effectively communicate, and

- will be successful.

DEALING WITH CONTROVERSY

Police "chiefing" is an unforgiving occupation. Ethical chiefs must sometimes take risks and endure controversy on behalf of the public good. It is rare for a police chief who has made significant accomplishments to avoid controversy. Sometimes during a selection process, a candidate must deal with a previous controversial situation. The key in a selection process is being able to effectively explain the situation and have supporting evidence (e.g., newspaper articles or editorials, and references who support your position).

In many instances, prior controversial issues that arise during a selection process only become controversial when they are kept hidden from the search committee and appointing authority. By being forthright in dealing with previous controversy, you can avoid having the matter become a serious issue. The last thing an appointing authority wants is to be blindsided by controversial information about a top candidate. Dealing directly with such issues early in the process provides the appointing authority time to review the issue and determine how big a factor it is in your candidacy. Given time to consider the issue when balanced with your overall qualifications, an appointing authority can sometimes devise a strategy for dealing with the issue as the process continues.

Dealing directly with the issues also gives the appointing authority confidence in your honesty and forthrightness. Be prepared to succinctly explain the issue and the environment surrounding it. Be careful not to blame others, and express confidence. Be instructive and remain unemotional. Your goal is to demonstrate the perspective you have gained from hard experience, not to reveal your bitterness, anger or frustration (self-deprecating humor can be essential). Try not to dwell on the subject, and be prepared to move on to the next subject.

As you advance in your career, controversies, votes of no confidence and political defeat become more likely. You must become your own reference library on these issues. If your position on an issue was ethical yet unpopular, this may be reflected in the newspaper coverage. This "objective" point of view can sometimes validate your position. Be careful never to "whine" in print over a controversy; maintain your professionalism. A newspaper article will become lasting documentation on the subject. Being on the losing end of an issue in a community known for "bare knuckles" politics can enhance your credibility in a more progressive community. Showing you can "take a hit" can also help you in more politically traditional communities.

Sometimes national and state contacts can be helpful in keeping local controversy in perspective. Generally speaking, the broader the perspective that is applied to a local controversy, the more ethical and appropriate an unpopular stand will appear. Your district attorney, attorney general, state training director, state association of chiefs, and contacts in Washington at IACP, PERF, and the Justice Department become very important.

How Can I Fail an Interview?

Losing out to your competition is just part of the job hunting game. But there is no excuse for beating yourself. Lack of preparation is the easiest way. Sloppy dress and grooming will do it. Poor posture, a limp handshake, a sloppy suit, nervous habits and smoking (even if the interviewers do) are sure ways to kill your chances. Bad manners and the use of offensive language are also sure losers. An off-color joke may get you a laugh, but it will probably lose you the job.

Criticism of your current employer reflects a lack of loyalty. Similarly, any criticism of the prospective department, even if you are certain every interviewer agrees with you, is very dangerous. At this point you are a visitor and an outsider, and you must show the appropriate deference to and respect for their community and police department. If you must be critical in the course of the interview, do it in a positive and constructive way.

Lack of clarity in presenting ideas, and the inability to convince the interviewer of your technical competence, will hurt you. Be cautious about expressing personal opinions on issues that might be sensitive to others. Stay clear of expressing opinions of a political or religious nature, even if it seems that the audience might be receptive. While it might engender solid support from some, you risk alienating others. If it is a consensus decision, you just lost.

Do not be late, do not oversell, and do not become overly confident. Give credit where credit is due. Few police administrators have been successful single-handedly.

At a lunch or dinner meeting, order moderately. At a lunch meeting, avoid ordering an alcoholic beverage. If it is a dinner interview, have no more than a single drink. Some people think you should not drink at all, but you will have to make a judgment call here. You want the interviewer to feel comfortable with you, so you will have to gauge each situation separately.

Recognize that you can fail an interview simply because the chemistry is not right. While it is strongly advocated that you do everything possible to prepare, the fact is that, no matter how good you are or how much you prepared, it may not be the right match. Do not agonize over the rejection. After all, it is a two-way street and an applicant has to feel equally at ease with the hiring authority. Capitalize on the process as a learning experience.

What Questions Can I Expect During an Interview?

Be prepared to answer certain questions during the interview. It is more difficult than you might think to succinctly respond to questions like "summarize your professional background" or "tell me what your career goals are." Most of the questions will deal with your past career and how you would deal with certain specific problems that the interviewing agency is facing. Generally speaking, there will be a greater emphasis on your management philosophy and style, as opposed to your technical skills.

You can count on being asked these six questions in one form or another:

1.   Summarize your professional and personal background.

2.   What have been your most important accomplishments?

3.   Why are you interested in this position?

4.   What strategies do you use to involve the community in decision making?

5.   What are your strengths and weaknesses?

6.   Where do you want to be professionally in five years?

While the preceding questions are perhaps the most common, be prepared to address all of the following issues:

- professional and personal background,

- concerns facing the police department,

- management and leadership style,

- knowledge of budgeting,

- crime strategies,

- experience with labor/management issues,

- examples of how you handle conflict,

- strategies for motivating employees,

- managing more with less,

- keeping the boss informed,

- effective strategies for communicating your message,

- training philosophy, and

- examples of decision making.

Finally, three additional questions have no right or wrong answer, but the responses may be extremely important to the hiring authority.

- If we consider you as our choice for police chief and ask past supervisors, subordinate employees, the news media and community leaders about you, what would they say?

- What questions do you have of us? What matters need further discussion?

- If you are offered the position, when would you be available? What are your salary expectations? Would we need to agree on any conditions of employment?

In addition to these general questions, be prepared to respond to specific issues that are currently of concern to the police department and the community. This is where your preparation for the interview pays off. Know what these issues are and, if you have not had firsthand experience with them, know what other police departments around the country are doing in these areas. This also allows you to showcase your knowledge of exemplary efforts at the national level, rather than just what has been happening in your own agency. If questioned about a specific plan of action on a particular issue, be cautious about committing yourself until you have more knowledge of how this issue specifically relates to this community. Rather, express your knowledge of the subject in terms of various strategies other agencies have used and what has proven successful. Committing to a specific action plan without sufficiently researching all of the factors can prove fatal.

You should also be prepared to answer questions regarding statistics related to your current organization. These include the population that your agency serves and its demographic breakdown, current crime statistics and any recent trends in crime, clearance rates, and the number of sworn and nonsworn personnel in your organization and their demographic breakdown. Interview committees often compare your operation with their own. If you do not know some of these numbers, you may be perceived as being too focused on your own area of command and not in touch with the big picture.

Find out who is on the interview committee before the interview. Anticipate each person's concerns and be prepared to address them. People who represent the business community will want to know about your thoughts in this area, and the same applies to those who represent the schools, churches and neighborhood groups.

RESPONDING TO QUESTIONS

Think about some of the best instructors you had in school or some of the best sermons you have heard. Most likely the speakers did not use abstract terms; they used a story or graphic description to make a point. The same applies to the interview. It is important to respond specifically to the question asked, but if you can make your point by illustrating it with examples, it has greater impact on the listener. As speech coaches and writing teachers say, "show, don't tell." Using a story to illustrate your point not only conveys specific experiences you have had, but keeps the interview interesting and the interviewer involved. It also helps the interviewer to remember you. An interviewer or interview committee often has a rigorous interview schedule. They may see as many as eight candidates in one day, many of whom may give the same general responses to the questions. Make a lasting impression on them by making your interview as interesting and informative as possible. Telling a story or illustrating with an example keeps your audience alert and centered on you. One word of caution, however—while it is important to give a graphic depiction of your capabilities, don't overshoot the time frame that has been allotted for your interview. Stay focused in your responses.

When preparing for the interview, you should not only anticipate certain questions, but think of the three to five main points about yourself that you want to convey during your interview. Be sure that you have clearly articulated why your experiences make you well qualified for this job. If the structured questions do not give you a chance to get these things on the table, try to make a closing statement before you leave to get these points across. You only get one chance to make these points, so make clear the strengths and capabilities you have for the job.

As you are posed questions in the interview, listen closely to what is being asked. Listening before responding is truly an art. Too often candidates assume they know the question, begin constructing a response, and miss a subtle aspect of the question. If the question asks for your experience, describe your experience. If it asks for your philosophy, explain your philosophy. If it asks how you would handle a situation, describe how you would handle it. Interviewers are generally adept at catching a candidate who avoids giving a direct answer to a question. Be succinct, but show that you have the necessary depth of knowledge on the given subject. This can be tricky. A good candidate will give a direct response to a question, illustrate the point and then stop talking. A good response to a question can lose its impact if the candidate begins to ramble. Police chief interviews frequently try to cover a lot of territory in a brief period of time. Not only do you have to cover a broad range of topics, but you have to retain the interviewer's interest. You may be asked what your thoughts are on 12 to 15 different subjects. Make your point and move on.

Be careful not to use the same general theme in responding to different questions. For instance, community policing, while central to much of police work, is not the answer to every question. Think outside the box.

YOUR QUESTIONS

The questions you ask during the interview are just as important as the answers you give. Asking questions not only shows that you are interested, but also gives you an opportunity to show what you know about the job and what type of professional you are. Prepare a short list of questions based on your pre-interview research. All questions should relate to the position. Do not ask about personal matters such as moving or schools; this is premature and should be posed at the follow-up interview. Concentrate on major management concerns that will affect your decision to accept or reject the job if it is offered to you. Who would you report to? How much authority would you have over personnel and budget issues? Are there concerns about the quality of the staff? What are the major departmental problems? In what direction would they like to see the department go? Do not ask about money. Long before the interview you should have determined (either with the recruiter or through your own research) that you are at least in the right "ballpark" as far as salary is concerned. Compensation details should be discussed only after a mutual interest has been established. Use your judgment as to the length of time that the committee has to field your questions. If they have a tight interview schedule, it may be in your best interest to keep this part of the interview brief and save additional questions for the follow-up interview. Also keep in mind the backgrounds of the people on the interview committee. Some of your questions may only be appropriate for the appointing authority, not the interview committee; save these questions for when you are alone with the appointing authority. However, you may ask questions related to committee members' specific community or city government concerns. This helps you establish a rapport with the committee members. If your committee is made up of community representatives, ask, "What are the community's expectations of a new police chief?"

CONCLUDING THE INTERVIEW

If you sincerely want the job, the most important thing you can do when the interview is winding down is to tell them just that: I really want this job! Too many people have not been offered jobs they really wanted because they simply did not convey they really wanted it. Leave on a friendly basis, having communicated your enthusiastic interest in the job. The saying "Last thing said, first thing remembered" often applies to the interview.

INTERVIEW FOLLOW UP

It is appropriate to formally acknowledge your appreciation for the interview. A typed thank you letter directed to the appointing authority or committee chairperson is proper etiquette following an interview. A brief, well-written note reinforces your continued interest in the position and your attention to detail.

Assessment Centers

WHAT IS AN ASSESSMENT CENTER?

Over the years, police departments have increasingly used the assessment center concept, although recently it has seen less use at the chief's level. An assessment center is a one- or two-day series of individual and group exercises designed to evaluate candidates' leadership, communications, interpersonal, management and analytical skills in a mock work environment. It is typically facilitated by a consultant who uses three or four trained observers. As a candidate, you would participate in a number of exercises requiring you to give a press conference, counsel a subordinate, prioritize and handle several matters in your in basket, write a report to council with only a little time, present a visual autobiography, or interact with your peers in some type of group situation.

In PERF's 1997 survey, 21.8 percent of chiefs reported that an assessment center was used in their selection process. The majority of chief selections are done without an assessment center. Some managers swear by them, and assessment center consultants obviously encourage their use as an evaluation tool. Some appointing authorities appreciate the opportunity to observe candidates in a group environment for an extended period of time.

If you are a candidate for a police chief position, be prepared to participate in an assessment center. Expect to be in three to five different exercises. Most of these will require you to role play. You will be faced with a problem and asked to resolve it in a defined period of time using defined resources. You may be involved in a group exercise with other candidates. You may have a written exercise, such as addressing various problems that are in your in basket. You may be asked to give a mock press conference or other presentation to an audience, and you may be asked to handle a meeting concerning a specific problem. Your behavior during these exercises will be observed and evaluated by trained assessors. The assessors rate each candidate based on predetermined criteria, and typically use benchmarks to help them in their evaluations. These assessors will then meet at the conclusion of the center and come to a consensus rating on each candidate.

HOW DO I PREPARE FOR AN ASSESSMENT CENTER?

- Be an assessor. If possible, take the opportunity to do this in advance of being a candidate. Understanding how the process works helps eliminate some of the anxiety.

- Know what behavioral dimensions are being used in your evaluation. If you know you are going to be evaluated on your judgment, leadership, decision-making ability and delegation, then be sure to display these strong aspects of your character.

- Clearly display your intentions during the center. The assessors cannot read your mind to know what you are thinking in a given situation. You must articulate your thoughts or indicate them in writing for the assessors to give you credit for your behaviors and actions.

- Most exercises allow you some time to prepare. Use this time wisely and develop a basic approach to handling the given situation. Know in advance what you want to accomplish in the exercise and stay with it. Maximize your preparation time.

- Get plenty of rest and reduce unnecessary sources of anxiety, such as not knowing how to get to the location of the center. Have a back-up alarm clock, and give yourself enough time to dress, eat and drive through traffic. Arriving late to the center will surely have a big impact on your performance.

- Pace yourself during the center. The process can be very draining. You need to show stamina and enthusiasm throughout the center. Candidates often start off strong in the first one or two exercises and then begin to drag as the day goes on. Try to maintain a consistent level of energy throughout the process.

- If you feel that you bombed on a certain exercise, try to get over it quickly so that it does not affect your performance in later exercises. Each exercise gives you a new opportunity to display your skills in different situations. It is likely that you can overcome a poor performance in one exercise if you perform very well in others.

- Usually, all of your notes will be collected by the assessors and used as part of their evaluation of your performance. Take thorough (and legible) notes that help support or explain your actions in the exercise. It may be helpful to make an outline of your plan.

- Good communication skills are essential to performing favorably in an assessment center. Not only do you need good speaking and writing skills, but listening and reading skills are also critical.

- The same general "rules of conduct" apply to assessment centers that apply to interviews in terms of appropriate body language, dress and communication. Eye contact is critical. Teaching experience is also a big help in assessment centers. Be yourself, and don't role play as someone with a different management style than your own.

- Wear a watch and be conscious of your time throughout the center. If you don't make your point in the allotted time, you lose the opportunity.

- You may be asked to use a flip chart or chalkboard to demonstrate aspects of your experience or a certain strategy. Know how to make an effective graphic display.

- Do a self-assessment before you are asked to participate in an assessment center. If you are weak in public speaking skills, get more experience. If you need to improve your writing skills, take a class on business writing. Practice staying focused on detailed information for a sustained period of time. These things can be helpful to you in your career as well as when competing for a job.

Here is some advice that might be helpful to you when giving assessment center presentations:

1. Define the issue or subject of the briefing.

2. Your briefings must have an introduction, a body of information and a summary.

3. Approach the topic confidently and deliver a succinct, attention-getting opening statement.

4. Briefings fail because of too much jargon, inappropriate or offensive words, and when nonverbal behavior conflicts with verbal behavior.

Watch your body language during the assessment center. Do not slouch in a chair or fidget. Do not put your hands on your face; it indicates hesitation, nervousness and insecurity. Do not tell jokes. Stay focused on each question or issue as it is presented to you.

Other Screening Methods

ESSAY QUESTIONS

To screen a group of candidates down to a short list of finalists, some cities ask candidates to respond to a set of essay questions. Typically applicants are asked to answer several questions and return their responses within a specified period of time (usually a week or two) for review by the appointing authority or other designated evaluators. The questions may relate to actual issues facing the department and community, or they may be much broader. Your responses are used to judge your knowledge on specific subjects, your attitude toward certain issues, your experience in different matters and your writing ability. The responses are compared with the appointing authority's profile for the ideal chief to determine whether or not each candidate stays in the process. The same guidelines apply in responding to these questions as apply to interview questions. You must do your homework, be knowledgeable on a broad range of police management issues, be conversant on trends in policing, be concise in your responses, and relate your experience to the issues in question. Some answers may be improved by reference to appropriate sources, such as research studies or articles. The ability to write well is an important attribute.

PSYCHOLOGICAL TESTING

Some cities contract the services of a psychologist to administer psychological or personality testing. This may involve written testing and/or interviews. This type of testing is designed to look at various aspects of your personality, how you interact with others, your management/communication style, and your approach to problem solving. Psychological testing is generally conducted toward the end of the process.

BACKGROUND INVESTIGATIONS

Just before, or soon after the interview, background investigations are generally conducted on candidates who are under serious consideration. These investigations may include only reference checking, or they may be full field investigations, including a review of all personnel files, internal affairs files, credit reports, tax records, criminal and civil court records, medical records, military records, college transcripts, and driving records; periodical searches; interviews with neighbors, spouses (current and former), domestic partners and current and past employers and supervisors; a national criminal records check; and an FBI clearance. You should anticipate this part of the process and be prepared to help facilitate it.

THE FOLLOW-UP INTERVIEW

The first thing to do if you are offered the job is to ask for a follow-up interview. If the job offer is bona fide, you should be allowed to return with your spouse for a follow-up interview to discuss the job more specifically.

This is your interview. Do not accept the job without going back to meet once more with the appointing authority. All too often a police executive will actually consider quitting a good job, relocating his or her family, and beginning a new job on the basis of a single interview with a person he or she met with for only an hour. Such behavior may be illogical, but it is common.

During the initial interview, the appointing authority was trying to pick the best candidate for the job. He or she asked most of the questions and eventually chose you. Now it is your turn. You are now in the "driver's seat," or as some have described it, the "window of opportunity" is now open. In the follow-up interview, ask the questions for which you need answers before you accept the job. During this interview, you want to get a better feel, not only for the job, but also for the person you will be working for. The advantage is yours now; use it when negotiating the terms of your employment.

PREPARING FOR THE FOLLOW-UP INTERVIEW

You prepare differently for the follow-up interview than you did for the first. Now is the time to address the details of salary, benefits, moving expenses, relocation costs or mortgage assistance, temporary housing, use of departmental vehicle, termination notice, severance pay, business expenses, civic memberships, vacation leave, outside employment, conference attendance, automobile and professional development.

Prepare a list of your current benefits, and make a list of additional things you would like to have. Combined, these two lists represent what you would like to have as conditions of employment—a point from which you can negotiate a contract. Remember, the window of opportunity does not stay open long. If you do not ask for the things that you need to be successful in this job, you probably will not get them. The appointing authority usually has a lot riding on your acceptance of an offer and will give you what you ask for if it is reasonable. An appointing authority usually does not want to have to begin negotiating with the second candidate on the list, and certainly does not want to start the entire process over again. Ask for the things that you will need while the timing is in your favor.

WHERE DOES YOUR SPOUSE FIT IN?

The follow-up interview allows you to discuss the important elements of the job offer. At the same time, your follow-up interview should provide your spouse with the opportunity to visit the community (especially if he or she did not visit at the initial interview) and look it over from the perspective of living there as well as a place of employment. Faced with the choice of accepting or rejecting the job offer, you and your spouse can assess the community in terms of the living environment.

During this second visit, you and your spouse should also consider the housing and school situation. Ask someone on the city staff to arrange for a meeting with school officials and a real estate agent. There is no sense in taking a new job, at least when you do not have to, if your family is not going to be satisfied with the community's schools or housing. As much as you may want this job, it is critical that your family be consulted and that they approve of the quality of life in that location. It is important that you schedule activities so that you and your spouse will have sufficient time to consider all aspects of the move.

Also tour the facilities in which you will be working. In particular, check out your future office. You are going to work long, hard hours in your office and if you want to make some improvements, now is the time to settle this issue. Once hired, it is amazing how hard things like office improvements and specialized equipment are to come by. A posh office is not a reason to accept a job, but you should be comfortable with your work environment. You will certainly spend enough hours in it.

7 | Projecting the Proper Image

A S PROFESSIONALS, we would like to believe that we will be judged by our professional qualifications and experience, as well as by what Martin Luther King called "the content of our character." But the truth is, people make initial impressions based on appearance, or "image." The saying "You never get a second chance to make a first impression" strongly applies to interviews.

Some studies have indicated that when you meet people, they judge you within the first minute. In that initial observation, people make judgments about your intelligence, competence and leadership abilities. Of course, these assessments are based on superficial information, but they nonetheless form distinct impressions.

Police executives, better than many, know the psychological impact and importance of a uniform. Yet they are often unaware of the image conveyed by an ill-fitting suit and a sloppy blouse or shirt. Enter any major corporation and you will see a dress code among managers. Leaf through any top corporation's annual report and note how the executives are dressed. The corporate world has recognized that one must "dress for success," and dozens of books have espoused the extra advantage a professional image gives. In the business world, professional dress is an occupational requirement. It is no different in policing.

Executive search consultants agree that a good appearance is necessary for an effective interview. One study has shown that interviewers make significant judgments during the first 40 seconds of an interview. Because you can hardly do more than say "hello" in that time, it is safe to assume the interviewers' assessment is determined by what they see.

It is difficult, then, to overestimate the importance of how you dress for an interview. Your appearance should reflect good taste, sound judgment and confidence—attributes any manager would find appealing. Your selection as a finalist tells you your credentials are in order. Beyond this point, your professional image can be one factor that gives you the edge over the other finalists. And the fastest way to rejection in the interview is through sloppy dress and grooming.

Dress must be appropriate for the occasion, the type of work you are applying for, and people with whom you interact. Because a police chief regularly works with professionals such as the mayor, city council members, judges, attorneys and local business people, he or she must dress in appropriate business attire. In an interview setting, proper dress shows appropriate respect to the interviewers.

Both men and women should be careful not to overdress or underdress for an interview. Underdressing signals to others that you lack sophistication and regard for your personal appearance. Overdressing may convey arrogance and a lack of sensibility. Finding the middle ground requires good judgment based on many factors, including the interviewers, the region and the city size.

You should not wear your uniform to an interview, even if you are an internal candidate and happen to be on duty the day of the interview. While many chiefs wear their uniforms once employed, it is not advisable in the interview because other candidates will be in business attire.

Men's Guide for an Interviewing Image

A suit must fit properly, regardless of how fashionable or expensive it is. If you do not have an appropriate suit that fits properly, buy a new one. It is a small investment to make for the chance to advance your career. Although men's fashions evolve, you cannot go wrong with a classically styled suit, with moderate lapels.

Although you can wear either a single- or double-breasted suit, in some circumstances, the latter might be too formal. Double-breasted jackets are fine for interviews, but are meant to be worn buttoned, which can be awkward when you sit down. Wear a dark colored suit (blue and gray are best), because darker colors tend to convey more authority and confidence. Avoid complicated plaid or checked patterns. You cannot go wrong with a traditionally tailored, solid or pin stripe, navy or charcoal gray suit. The fabric should be appropriate to the season and the climate where you are interviewing. Pleated trousers have an updated look and wrinkle less than plain-front trousers. Trouser cuffs are a matter of personal preference. A blazer or sport coat is not appropriate for a chief's interview. Some people like to wear a handkerchief in the breast pocket. This might be considered overly formal for an interview. If it is done, the handkerchief and tie should never match, but should coordinate well.

Wear a solid white, mostly or all cotton, long-sleeved shirt, and have it professionally laundered and starched. It should fit properly, not only in size, but also in cut, and should show no signs of wear. Straight collars have become more common and give a more formal look. Use collar stays so the collars do not curl up. Button-down collars are acceptable, but give a slightly more casual look. If wearing a shirt with a French cuff, wear a simple gold or silver cuff link. Be aware that cuff links may make you look overdressed in some places.

A silk tie is a must. The best design choices are subtle, conservative prints such as foulards, stripes or small dots with colors that complement your suit. A tie that has red in it works well. Avoid ties that are exceptionally bright or bold, so the design does not distract from your presentation. If you have not bought a new tie in several years, now is the time. The tie should be long enough to reach the belt line. Avoid wearing tie clips, tie bars and tie tacks, especially one carrying the ever-popular miniature handcuff motif.

Business suits generally require a belt. The best approach is to match the belt to your shoes. Wear black with blue or gray suits, and brown belts with brown suits. Your belt buckle should be plain and simple. Button-on braces, while somewhat less conservative, are increasing in popularity, and are acceptable to wear to an interview in lieu of a belt. Never wear both. Do not wear suspenders with alligator clips.

Dark leather dress shoes in black, brown or cordovan should be polished and in good condition. They should have a thin sole. Don't wear a casual slip-on style such as a loafer. A good quality lace-up leather wing tip style is best. Black shoes go with a black, navy or gray suit, brown shoes go with brown and olive, and cordovan goes with almost anything. Under no circumstances should you wear the corfam, military-style (shiny black plastic) dress shoe. Wear thin, neat dark dress socks. The general rule is to ensure your socks are darker than your suit. Be sure they are the over-the-calf style so that when you cross your legs, your bare leg does not show.

Coats—both trench coats and overcoats—should be classically styled, reach below the knee, and fit comfortably over your suit. A shade of beige, tan, olive, navy or gray is good for the trench coat, while navy, gray or camel is a good choice for the overcoat.

Jewelry should be limited. Wear a thin analog (not digital) watch in gold or silver. An expensive watch often catches attention in an interview and may convey extravagance. Limit rings to a wedding band and signet ring.

Women's Guide for an Interviewing Image

As with men's attire, women's clothing should be simple and tailored, and not distract the interviewer. The message a woman's appearance should convey in an interview is, "I'm in control."

When you are meeting with someone new in a business setting, conservative dress is always best. Choose a suit that is skirted, classically styled, fully lined and long-sleeved. Your suit should fit well and be of good quality. It should be updated in style, but conservative. Of all the styles, the single-breasted suit is the most formal and conservative. Combined with a straight skirt, this look projects authority and confidence. Choose suit fabrics carefully. Avoid linen, rayon and any other fabrics that wrinkle easily. Choose fabric appropriate for the season and climate where the interview takes place. Solids, tweeds and subtle plaids work best. Avoid pinstripes; they tend to resemble the look of a man's suit.

The same rules of color for men apply to women. The darker the color, the more authority and confidence is projected and therefore, shades such as charcoal gray, black, olive, taupe or burgundy are good choices. Some employment experts say that a subtle yet more "interesting" shade, such as plum or dark red, can help a woman to appear confident and self-assured. Beige and lighter blues are professional looks for the office, but may not impart the level of confidence you need in an interview. Navy suits may look too much like a uniform.

Your skirt should fall at or slightly below the knee. A shorter skirt, although fashionable, does not project the proper interview image. Stockings should be sheer, not white or black.

If you prefer to wear a dress, it should be tailored similar to a suit and follow the same guidelines for style, color, length and fabric that are outlined above. Never wear pant suits or slacks to an interview.

Your shoes should have a medium heel and be polished. Plain leather pumps are best. High heels and flats do not work in an interview. Avoid carrying a handbag, if possible. If it is necessary to carry one, it should be small, neat, complement your shoes and be of good quality. Do not carry both a handbag and a briefcase.

Accessories should not interfere with your overall look. Keep them to a minimum. The "Rule of Seven" dictates that you should have no more than seven points of interest on your body at a given time. Your jewelry or scarves should complement your outfit, but not command too much attention. Blouses should be plain and neat in appearance. A classic shell works well under a suit. Stay away from bright colors, ruffles, low necklines and big prints. If you wear nail polish, choose clear. Keep make-up simple. If an overcoat is necessary, it should cover the length of your skirt and be of good quality and classic styling.

Because women have many more choices than men when it comes to interview attire, it can be much more difficult to decide on your overall look. When in doubt, get the advice of another female executive.

Finishing Touches

Avoid wearing lapel pins or other jewelry that indicates some political, religious or other affiliation.

It is not necessary to bring a briefcase, unless you are asked to bring materials with you to the interview. However, if you need to carry one, it should be leather and very neat in appearance. You may want to carry a leather portfolio for extra résumés and notepaper. Carry a good quality pen, and a back-up pen just in case.

When preparing your interview attire, pay special attention to your shoes. Some people take particular note of the condition of shoes, so be sure they are properly polished. Details like these can make a difference, so anticipate them.

Take enough clothes for the entire interview trip. If the trip is going to entail an interview, dinner and a follow-up interview the next day, you should bring two suits. If you are flying to the site, try to carry your luggage on the plane to avoid the risk of losing it.

If you are interviewing locally or internally, you should not bring your portable police radio to the interview, and you should certainly never leave it on. The interviewers deserve your full, undivided attention.

Finally, you need to feel good about the way you look in the interview. You will reflect the way you feel in your body language, and ultimately in the way you communicate your confidence to the interviewers. The objective with interview attire is to convey an updated yet conservative, professional appearance, so that the interviewers focus on you and what you have to say, not your wardrobe.

CHAPTER 7

8 | Effective Negotiations

N EGOTIATION—the process of reaching agreement—should be deliberate and straightforward. In this important step, you and the employer will determine your rights and responsibilities in the new position, establish expectations and set compensation. You and the appointing authority should first explore what is important in the employment relationship, and then discuss how you might reach consensus. Although each person will negotiate in a way he or she feels comfortable, this brief overview will provide some basic principles to consider as you work toward agreement.

The Power Shift

Throughout the search process, the appointing authority is in the position of power as he or she winnows the number of candidates down to a single one. However, once an offer is made to the final candidate, the power position begins to shift toward the candidate. This power shift occurs during the limited window of opportunity during which you will negotiate terms of employment, such as a compensation package and other contract provisions.

This power shift occurs for two important reasons. First, the search process has likely been going on for about six months, garnering a fair amount of public attention and city resources. Once the appointing authority decides that you are his or her choice, rejection of the offer would be a major problem. Many times, there is a number-two candidate waiting in the wings; however, the appointing authority usually does not want to go to plan B. Worse yet, there may not be a number two, and the only option is to conduct another search. If it is public knowledge that the offer has been made, a rejection reflects poorly on the appointing authority.

The second reason for this power shift is that the selection of a police chief will be the most important appointment the city manager or mayor will make. The chief's performance and ultimate success or failure will reflect directly on the appointing authority.

The time to negotiate for the things that you need to be successful is now. Once the deal is done, you cannot go back and ask for more, at least not with the same power balance in your favor. You have a limited window of opportunity to get the compensation that you and your family will be comfortable with, the authority necessary to make organizational decisions that lead to success, and the protections that will allow you to make those decisions without concern for political interference that could jeopardize your job security.

A word of caution: this power shift puts you in a position to negotiate with confidence, not arrogance. A shrewd appointing authority will not hesitate to withdraw an offer if during the negotiations he or she observes previously unseen behaviors that indicate future difficulty in the relationship.

Good Faith

The way you negotiate conditions of employment is your first employee-supervisor relations "test." Negotiation will leave impressions that will affect all future relations you have with your new supervisor and other hiring authorities. Ideally, these negotiations will lay a foundation of trust and confidence. Negotiations that prove difficult or acrimonious may be an important sign that you should reconsider the offer. Good relationships with the boss are crucial to occupational success.

"Be yourself" is essential advice in all phases of the recruitment and selection process. During negotiations the "real you," your style, your approach to problem solving, your articulation of ways to deal with sensitive issues, and the openness with which you deal with the negotiation process will establish your future relationship with the appointing authority.

The ideal ingredients for employment negotiations are similar to those that make for success in policing—integrity, respect, self-confidence, straightforward presentation, support of your position and convictions, open exchange, and respect for the views and expressions of all parties. Ideally, the negotiation process should be a "win-win" situation, concluded in an atmosphere of mutual respect and enthusiasm to move forward together in service to the community.

Getting Started

Often there is a feeling of awkwardness about "getting down to terms." The candidate must be prepared to introduce and guide the discussion, particularly when dealing with a young or inexperienced manager or mayor. Without being overbearing or condescending, you should not take for granted that the employer has a thorough understanding of negotiating contracts.

An effective way to initiate negotiation is to provide the appointing authority with an easily understandable copy of your current salary and a complete list of benefits. This provides a clear understanding of your present compensation package, which can be reviewed with the expectation of increased or expanded salary and benefits.

In initially presenting your conditions for employment, be complete. Appointing authorities typically become impatient, uncomfortable and eventually unforgiving of a candidate who presents conditions one or two at a time, and seems always to have one more item to discuss. Get every bit of it on the table, conceptually at least, and then deal with the specifics.

Bear in mind that what may appear as resistance to a particular benefit may stem from misunderstanding, not refusal to negotiate. Confusion or misunderstanding, often not readily spoken, can impede, or even prevent, continuing productive negotiation. It is imperative that you be both a good explainer as well as a good listener throughout negotiation discussions.

How Much is Too Much?

Everything that is important to you should be placed "on the table." Obviously, reason, honesty and compromise should prevail during any negotiation about employment. The positions of both parties should be thoughtfully discussed, but you should never be reluctant to emphasize your years of experience and proven abilities.

You have an established career track record of achievement in police services. You have defined and verifiable abilities to offer an organization—that's why you are the finalist. Do not be either overly modest or overbearing. In a forthright manner, present your potential usefulness and commitment to the job. In addition, do not be reluctant to present your personal needs, your responsibilities to your family and any other important requirements. The negotiation session is the time to fully represent your worth in terms of money and related benefits that can be "totaled up." Rest assured that the appointing authority has already considered the expected compensation package that must be offered to place you in the chief's office. In the world of municipal salaries and public budgets, it is unlikely that there will be a vast disparity between what you ask for and what the appointing authority can offer. After all, there will be enough surprises during your tenure. There should be few with regard to initial and projected compensation and personal worth.

The Wrap-Up

The recruitment process can be long and arduous for all involved. Following interviews of candidates, most managers are disposed toward making an appointment decision quickly. They are likely to presume you are similarly disposed to make a quick response to an appointment offer. You ought to be prepared to say "yes" or "no" as soon as is reasonably possible, but time is needed to write up the conditions that are agreed upon during the negotiation.

Make sure that you have discussed the details of the negotiations and employment conditions with your family before accepting any offer. You do not want to get the appointing authority to agree to all of your terms only to have your family say no.

If you truly want the position, you may secure it with an immediate good-faith handshake and the promise of a prompt meeting to sign the agreement and make mutual public announcements of your appointment. Usually the appointing authority is exhilarated over the completion of a major task and especially "high" on having hired a new police chief. Any subsequent delays, new conditions or surprises will nearly always result in disappointment, and can erode a relationship that has not even yet begun. Negotiate in good faith, establish conditions fair to both parties, do sufficient homework and personal deliberation to be able to say "YES!" to an appointment offer, and get on the new job as soon as is reasonably possible. That is the ideal wrap-up of any negotiation!

In summary, there are four steps you should take if offered a job:

1. Request reasonable time to discuss the offer with your family and prepare a list of your conditions for acceptance. One week should be enough.

2. Present your conditions of employment to the appointing authority. Be able to defend each condition.

3. Modify your requirements to the extent possible.

4. Reach agreement and reduce the major items to writing.

Use the following sample checklist to guide negotiations.

Sample Negotiating Checklist

	Current Benefit	Proposed
Salary	$79,000	$89,000
Pension	Defined benefit	10% contribution to 401(a) and use of 457 Plan
Automobile	Duty take-home	Leased—$350/mo. allowance
Life insurance	$25,000	2 1/2 times salary
Health insurance	Family	Family and orthodonture provision
Vacation	Three weeks	Four weeks
Sick leave	10 days	12 days
Comp time	Reasonable	Reasonable
Business expenses	Reasonable	Reasonable
Conferences	one/year	two/year—national two/year—in-state
Moving	None	Packing, moving and storage Househunting expenses (two trips with spouse)
Outside employment options	None	Up to one week of outside consulting
Executive development program	None	Extended paid leave of absence available

Tips for Negotiating

Deal with the whole package. Compensation is made up not only of salary, but also employee benefits and job security. Consider the total package as you negotiate based on your present situation.

Protect severance. This is the most important and valuable component of the employment agreement. Language regarding severance should be unambiguous and legally sound.

Do your homework. Know the cost to the employer of the items you are negotiating so that you can effectively customize a package that works best for you. Some cities may have financial, political or legal limitations that restrict the appointing authority's ability to agree to certain benefits, compensation or conditions of employment.

Understand what these are, and be creative to come to an agreement.

Negotiate only with the person who has settlement authority. There will be a better understanding of the issues on both sides, and you will come to closure faster if you work out the details of the contract directly with the appointing authority.

Do not overreach. Negotiate reasonably and in good faith. Remember that the tone of your future relationship begins here.

Document each resolved point. Negotiations may become complex and can be simplified by documenting each point as it is agreed upon.

Do not bluff. It should go without saying that if you bluff, you might lose everything.

Consider compensation over the long term. When a new police chief comes to town, much attention is often focused on the starting salary. This can instigate public and internal criticism that is hard to overcome. Consider forms of compensation that automatically increase over time, such as guaranteed salary increases with favorable performance, a generous amount of annual leave that can be cashed out on separation, or a higher employer contribution to a tax-deferred annuity plan. These areas are less likely to generate public attention.

Segregate issues. While it is important to negotiate a total package, some items (such as a portable pension fund versus a standard pension plan) should be isolated to make it easier to reach agreement. Some items may require specific discussion, and your ability to explain well can become critical.

Be patient. Both sides benefit if sufficient time is given to both planning for the negotiation sessions, and the actual negotiating. When the process is rushed, items can be left out that either side may regret later.

Offer solutions. Think creatively if negotiations stall. Your ideas are more likely to have greater benefit to you than the appointing authority's ideas.

Keep the sessions short. With proper planning and the ability to explain how provisions benefit all parties involved, the negotiations should be kept simple and you should be able to move quickly through a series of short meetings.

Be prepared to trade. Know in advance what items cannot be compromised and those that can.

Be able to walk away. If the deal does not provide the tools to be successful in the job, as well as satisfy your personal and family needs, walk away. If you accept a job that does not make you feel good, then it is not a good career move.

CHAPTER 8

9 | Compensation

Salary

A new chief's salary will be determined by a number of factors, the most important of which is probably what comparable jurisdictions are paying their police chiefs. Other factors include how much the applicant is earning in his or her present position, how much the former chief was paid, the city's pay plan, how badly the manager wants the applicant, local politics, and the strength of the applicant's negotiating skills.

One good source of information is the current issue of *Police Salaries* published by the International City/County Management Association (ICMA). These are drawn from ICMA's annual compensation survey of local government salaries and benefits. The data are generally one year old—this year's issue will show the previous year's survey. As you review the statistics, you will note some geographic variation in salary and benefits. For example, jobs in the Pacific Coast states are generally higher paying, while lower paying positions are found in the South and South Central states. This information may help you, not only in your future planning, but also in determining where you might or might not be willing to apply for a position. To view the entire ICMA compensation survey, including all municipal positions, check in a city administrator's office or a good library. Additionally, state municipal leagues and state police chief organizations may produce regional surveys.

Employee Benefits

Employee benefits, along with salary, make up the total compensation package. Too often candidates focus solely on salary, not recognizing that benefits are a critical part of the total compensation package. The cost of a good benefit package will be about 30 to 50 percent of your salary. Therefore, you should carefully evaluate the benefit package when considering a job change. For example, if you are within a year or so of becoming vested in a retirement program, it may not be wise to change jobs, even though you will receive a substantial salary increase. This increase may be offset by losses in pension benefits. Ideally, any new employment situation should at least match your current job's benefits.

Too often, executives successfully negotiate a salary increase, yet are content to accept the standard employee benefit package. As in salary negotiating, you should bargain for a generous, yet fair and reasonable benefit package before accepting a position. If the employer cannot offer you the salary you want, the government entity may be willing to offset the salary limitation with a better benefit package. Even after you are hired, consider attempting to improve your benefit package each year, even if you do little more than add a few thousand dollars of life insurance coverage.

There are two advantages to building up your benefit package annually. The first is obvious—you improve your quality of life. The second is less obvious but also important. By improving your package with your current employer, you increase the probability of securing a solid benefit package with future employers, because employers frequently consider salary histories in devising salary and benefit offers.

Pension and Deferred Compensation Programs

While many compensation specialists feel that a pension is the most important benefit for long-term security, it often escapes the mobile police chief. While many chiefs are covered by state or city retirement plans, some specifically for police and/or fire employees, these plans frequently require a number of years of participation to vest. By moving from job to job, perhaps state to state, the police chief may fail to accrue enough time in any one position to become vested in a pension program. For example, some plans may require a career of 30 years to fully vest. Other plans partially vest in a shorter period. For example, the California state plan requires a participant to be employed as a police officer in the state for five years to receive some retirement benefit.

So if you plan to consider opportunities in other agencies, it is important that you have a portable retirement plan. There are a variety of these plans, sometimes called deferred income or deferred compensation plans. This type of plan generally allows an employer and/or employee to make before-tax contributions to a retirement fund that may be invested in a choice of investment options, such as long-term growth equity funds, income-oriented bond funds or low-risk guaranteed return funds. The key to these plans is that one can reduce current tax exposure by diverting otherwise taxable income into a fund that accumulates without tax liability until withdrawal around age 60, when presumably income levels, and corresponding tax rates, are lower.

We refer to these plans by their Internal Revenue Code designation. A 401(a) plan, called a money purchase plan, is common for government employers. Typically, the employer makes regular contributions to the plan, and the employee may make a contribution as well up to a total of the lesser of $30,000 or 25 percent of taxable income. (Similar 401(k) plans are intended for profit-making entities, although a few public employers may still retain a "grandfathered" plan.) Premature withdrawals before age 59 $1/2$ will trigger a penalty.

Deferred compensation plans (also known as 457 plans) allow an employee to divert current otherwise taxable income into a retirement plan. Employers generally do not contribute to 457 plans. The employee may contribute up to about $8,000 per year. These plans are considered supplemental so that a public employee may contribute the maximum amount to a 401 plan and still make 457 plan contributions. There is also a withdrawal provision allowing you to remove funds early without penalty under certain circumstances.

Thus, the mobile chief who seeks a position in a jurisdiction with a pension plan that requires years of vesting should negotiate for both a 401(a) plan, with a contribution from the city, and the option to participate in a 457 plan. The city's contribution amounts can vary from 2 to 3 percent to more than 10 percent gross salary. You should note, however, that contributors on the low end may also sponsor mandatory defined contribution plans, so the 401(a) is only a supplemental plan. The higher end contributing cities may offer only a single 401(a) option and no other plan.

Not all jurisdictions sponsor 401 and 457 plans, so they may be items to negotiate. Consider including a retirement plan provision in your contract or letter of agreement. Keep in mind that cities can set up plans for an entire class of employees or a single employee, and the administrative cost to the city is minimal.

Of course there are other options you should pursue to ensure a secure retirement, assuming you have ample disposable income. Making annual contributions to an Individual Retirement Account (IRA) is a sensible way to augment pension funds.

Rules on retirement plans are complex and ever changing, and individual needs vary. As a result, you should seek professional guidance from a qualified financial planner or tax advisor if necessary. For additional information, you might contact one of the companies that manages retirement plans. The International City/County Management Association

(ICMA) Retirement Corporation administers plans for many city governments and can be a very good source of information.

Retirement comes more quickly than you expect. The earlier you set up a portable retirement plan or a deferred compensation plan, the more secure your retirement will be, and the better prepared you will be for future employment opportunities.

Automobile

An allowance for an automobile, whether for work-related commuting, personal use or both, significantly increases your disposable income. The American Automobile Association recently calculated that the average cost of operating a car is almost $5,500 per year, or $458 per month. The average U.S. household spends nearly one-fifth of its income on a vehicle and related costs, according to the U.S. Bureau of Labor Statistics. The figure rises significantly for full-size cars and sport utility vehicles. If you can negotiate for the right to use an employer-owned car, obtain a leased vehicle or receive a car allowance, for business, personal and family use, you may eliminate the need for a second car and its associated costs. Of course, there is a tax liability for the value of the benefit you receive when you make personal, rather than business, use of the car.

There are essentially three ways to structure a vehicle benefit provision. First, there is the direct use of a car from the employer's fleet. The second, and perhaps most attractive option for the employee, is to lease a vehicle. A leased vehicle makes it clear to others that the use of the vehicle is a benefit and not simply a job-related piece of equipment on loan from the city. Also, leased vehicles are usually more comfortable and better equipped. The arrangement may simply provide for a monthly lease allowance and allow you to select the car. Third, you may have to negotiate for reimbursement for the use of your own vehicle, either on a fixed monthly fee basis, which is preferable, or a per mile reimbursement. In any case, try to ensure there is an annual escalator amount built into the agreement. If a car is required in your daily administrative activities, determine what it will cost you to operate the car on a monthly basis, and then request that amount of reimbursement. If you are not reimbursed for the use of your personal car for necessary job-related activities, then you are losing money. Remember that personal use of an employer-provided car will require you to report the value of the benefit as income.

Beyond the financial benefits of securing some subsidy for the use of an automobile, appropriate financial arrangements in a contract or agreement may prevent an embarrassing situation, such as if you were to be found using your city car for a personal reason.

Insurance

Four types of insurance coverage should concern you—health, life, disability income and professional liability. In most instances, it is difficult to obtain a health and medical insurance package different than the one offered to other employees in the agency. However, you should determine whether or not the coverage offered by your prospective employer is adequate.

If a member of your family has, or will have, the need for special medical treatment, be sure you consider this when changing jobs. Orthodontic work on a couple of teenagers can wipe out a significant salary increase if you lose your dental insurance in a job switch. Coverages for mental health care or elective procedures, such as cosmetic surgery, can vary as well. Compare deductibles, the employee share of premiums for the employee and family, and the type of care provided, whether it is a health maintenance organization, a preferred provider plan or a more traditionally structured plan.

Insurance coverage will be terminated when you change jobs unless you exercise your right under COBRA, a federal law that continues insurance coverage for separating employees. The employee is responsible for paying the premiums to a third party administrator, but it is probably the best option if coverage under the new employer's policy is not effective for some time after the employment begins. This allows you to retain the same health care providers. Another option is to buy short-term coverage, although it tends to be expensive. You may choose instead to purchase a short-term major medical or catastrophic medical policy, which protects you from serious financial loss, but offers little or no compensation for minor or routine medical costs. In any case, be sure you have adequate coverage between jobs.

If the employing agency does not offer a generous term life insurance package, you should negotiate for this benefit. Term life insurance means that there is a death benefit for named beneficiaries if the insured dies. It is distinguished from a whole life or universal life policy, which builds cash value over the course of many years, while simultaneously providing a modest death benefit. These policies are a conservative way to save for retirement while also offering some life insurance protection. Cities generally provide only term coverage.

Typically, you will be offered whatever a specific employee group (usually department heads) receives. However, unlike medical and health insurance, the municipality can increase life insurance coverage with ease. All it has to do is buy more, and since it is purchased under a group rate, it is a fairly inexpensive benefit. The more life insurance your employer provides, the less you may have to carry privately. If at all possible, always purchase insurance that guarantees portability. This will allow you to carry the package with you throughout your career. It becomes more difficult to qualify for and obtain adequate life insurance as you advance in age, because the risk of premature death increases. Life insurance premiums paying for coverage of $50,000 or more will be imputed as income, according to IRS regulations, but it is a relatively minor expense compared with the peace of mind that you have adequate coverage to protect your family. Of course you should always investigate the option of buying additional coverage independently, as it can be more cost effective.

Disability income protection insurance provides you with some percentage of your monthly income, should you become disabled. Policies are both short-term, effective soon after being disabled, and long-term, where a typical package guarantees the employee 50 percent of his or her salary, starting 90 days after a disabling accident or illness. (Be sure the policy does not call for reduced payments in Social Security benefits.) Only some municipalities provide this coverage as part of their standard insurance package. Without this type of coverage, you risk a serious financial loss if you are forced out of work because of a debilitating accident or illness.

To convince your employer that this type of insurance is a reasonable job requirement, argue that at one time or another, we have all been faced with what to do when a valuable employee can no longer work because of an illness or accident. In most situations, we try to keep the employee on the payroll for as long as possible. Ultimately, we are forced to "bite the bullet" and terminate the employee. When a person is covered by disability income protection insurance, termination is easier for all involved. If you are unable to convince your employer to obtain this type of insurance for you, then buy it yourself—it's that important! Paying the premium yourself does have tax benefits, should you make a claim. For example, if you paid 60 percent of the premium, then 60 percent of any claim money would be yours tax-free.

Adequate professional liability insurance should be part of any benefit package. It should not be considered optional, but an absolute requirement for the job. Without this coverage, you risk financial disaster should you be sued individually. The coverage should be comprehensive, including protection from potential claims, from employees alleging wrongful discharge, to arrestees alleging officers' excessive use of force. Liability policies generally will not cover a chief's intentional or unlawful misconduct, but will provide protection against claims of negligence. Considering the frequency of litigation against police chiefs, the potential for very large awards to successful plaintiffs, and the type of decisions you must make daily, this insurance is an absolute necessity. Any policy, even if you are to be covered on the general city policy, should be reviewed to ensure that its exclusions are reasonable, and that it provides adequate protection against common claims a chief might face.

Annual Physical and Executive Medical Plan

Ask your employer to provide you with a complete annual medical examination. You owe it to both yourself and your employer to be in the best possible physical condition. An annual physical will contribute to this goal. Further, as a preventive measure, it could reduce costs to your employer and your insurance carrier. Since this cost is not normally covered, you might also negotiate an executive medical plan that covers not only health, but also dental and other uncovered health care costs up to a fixed amount per year.

Vacations

If you are not careful, you could lose vacation benefits in a job change. You may leave a position where, due to long tenure, you have "maxed out" the leave benefit, and assume a job with entry-level vacation benefits. Ideally, a new employer will meet or beat the leave allowance of the former employer. At the very least, request at least three weeks of vacation per year to start. You should also ask that some portion be credited in advance so that you are not precluded from taking time off early in your tenure. Because of the long hours you are required to work, and the difficulty you might have in finding time to be away from work at all, try to negotiate the ability to accumulate an unlimited amount of vacation time. You also want to be compensated for any accrued time when you leave the job. In some situations, it may be the only severance pay you are going to receive.

Sick Leave

Try to start off with a credit of at least 30 sick days as a hedge against any possible serious illness. Because sick leave is usually accumulated at about one day per month, you could find yourself in a difficult financial position if you become seriously ill during the first year or two of employment. Even if you have disability income protection insurance, it may only offer long-term coverage, and become effective 60 to 90 days after you leave work.

The best way to convince your employer of the need for this type of benefit is to point out that you have always accumulated a considerable amount of sick leave with your previous employers (assuming you have), and that you require such protection before accepting a new job offer.

Compensatory Time

PERF's survey found that police chiefs often work a 60-hour week. Typically, a police chief will spend the daytime hours leading and administering the organization, followed by evening meetings with the city council, other government organizations, public interest groups and associations, and just about anyone else wanting a portion of the chief's time. Long hours are unavoidable as a police chief executive. Although a chief is classified as an "exempt" employee, and not entitled to overtime pay, the reasonable use of compensatory time in lieu of vacation days is probably justified. Be sure that you and your employer agree on what is reasonable.

Severance Pay

Severance provisions provide an employee with some compensation, usually equal to several months or years of salary, in the event the employment relationship is terminated by the employer before the end of an agreed-upon term (usually three, four or five years). The employer's agreement to pay severance serves as an inducement to retain your services for a specific period. If your employer wants you to risk a job change, expects you to shoulder the associated costs of assuming the new position, and wants a long-term commitment from you, he or she should be willing to reciprocate by granting a severance package. Should you negotiate a severance provision, you will likely be obligated to remain in the position for the full term of the contract unless the agreement is terminated prematurely. Be sure to review the applicable provisions that govern termination so you know the consequences should you decide to leave the position before the contract expires.

Business Expenses

Be sure that you have a clear understanding with your prospective employer about business expenses. Your employer should reimburse you for any reasonable business-related expenses, such as required job-related lunch and dinner meetings. This can be a touchy subject, because public opinion is not always understanding of the need for some sort of allowance. If your expense provision is not agreed on before your employment, you may find yourself in an embarrassing predicament if you later try to obtain reimbursement. Membership in local civic organizations and professional organizations that either directly further your effectiveness in the community, or promote your professional development, should be paid for by your employer, but use good sense when requesting reimbursement. About 95 percent of the chiefs responding to the PERF survey reported that the city paid for professional memberships.

Conference Attendance, Training and Education

Before you accept a position, determine which professional conferences you will be allowed to attend and what expenses will be covered, and confirm that attendance days will not be charged against vacation days. It is standard practice for cities to pay for chiefs to attend professional conferences; the PERF survey showed that 97 percent of the responding chiefs received reimbursement for travel expenses, including conference registration fees. You may consider requesting the option of taking your spouse with you to a conference at the employer's expense. Some city managers or mayors will agree that, for an appropriate conference, travel expenses are justified.

Employers should make time and financial allowances for training and education. A chief should be able to attend two or three training sessions per year, each typically one or two days, to keep pace with changes in the profession, upgrade technical skills and perhaps maintain professional certifications. You may want to request time and financial support for more academically focused opportunities, so long as they benefit your professional development and ultimately improve your ability to perform for the department and city. An occasional return to the classroom and exposure to an academic environment is an excellent way to recharge your batteries and engage in creative thinking.

Many communities will be reluctant to allow a chief to take significant time away. But it is possible. One chief from a Western resort community secured authorization from his city manager to attend the FBI National Academy by obtaining a slot during the off-season when his community and department were less busy. He also had a trusted commander who could step in and lead the agency in his absence. But a city prepared to give that much time away, with full pay, is unusual. While it may not be appropriate to raise the issue of extended absences with a prospective employer during negotiations, at the very least you ought to review the city's educational leave and tuition assistance policies.

A leave of absence without pay is one option if a city is reluctant to continue to pay salary. One commander took advantage of a leave of absence from his department and enhanced his educational credentials significantly by earning a master's degree in public administration from Harvard University's Kennedy School of Government. Soon after graduation, he took a chief's position in a medium-sized Midwest city.

Of course, the best option is to secure extended educational opportunities when you are in a command position, and before you take a chief's job.

Moving Expenses

The transportation of your household goods is only part of the cost of moving. However, frequently the employer is thinking only of what it will cost to hire the movers. The cost of moving includes packing and unpacking, transportation of your household goods, meals and lodging for the family while traveling, temporary accommodations, expenses while househunting, realtor fees and other miscellaneous costs. These expenses will very quickly eat up a salary increase. In the private sector, these costs are frequently passed on to the employer. Today, most city managers recognize that a new chief should receive some reimbursement.

Securing a new mortgage with its required service charges means that the cost of moving is substantial. This problem is compounded if you are caught buying in a seller's market and selling in a buyer's market. If a salary increase will not sufficiently compensate for these costs, you should consider alternatives. One option is a flat relocation fee, while another is that the municipality obtains a favorable mortgage for you. Another option is for the employer to buy your house, or provide you with a monthly subsidy until your house is sold. Because these are not standard benefits, you will probably not get them unless you make them a condition of your employment.

Only limited types of moving costs qualify for a tax deduction if your employer does not reimburse them. Fully deductible costs include moving your household goods, and travel expenses to your new home. If your employer does not reimburse you for these expenses, be sure to file IRS Form 3903.

Hidden Costs

Carefully analyze how your benefits, the cost of living and housing costs compare before you accept a new job. A sizable salary gain can be negated by the difference in housing costs, mortgage rates, salary deductions for Social Security and employer pension contributions. For example, housing costs vary drastically across the United States. A 1998 survey revealed that, while the median sale price of a home in the Buffalo, N.Y., area was $84,000, the median sale price of a home in the San Jose area was $317,000. In other words, a move from one area to another could cost you in disposable income.

Your net income can be profoundly affected by a change in your benefits. Let us assume in your current job you are not making Social Security contributions, your family medical insurance is fully covered, and you are contributing 5 percent of your salary to a pension plan. You then take a new job where you are required to make Social Security contributions, pay for your family medical insurance and contribute 7 percent to the pension fund. These changes can cost you $300 to $500 per month. The practical effect is reducing your disposable income by $3,600 to $6,000 annually.

Chapter 9

10 | Employment Agreements and Contracts

EMPLOYMENT AGREEMENTS or contracts are becoming increasingly common between local governments and their top administrators, and you should consider securing one. You may hear, "It's never been done here before," "It will set a precedent for other department heads," "The city council will not buy into it," and "The city charter prevents it." But with some creativity, good counsel and logical arguments, you may find agreement. PERF's survey found that 26 percent of chiefs had a contract, and the trend toward contracts appears to be growing.

As community-based policing is now the norm in many communities, the police chief's job has become increasingly more complex. There are higher expectations for the chief's performance from a multitude of constituencies, both inside and outside the agency. Many more people today are involved in the subjective evaluation of the chief from different points of view. This creates greater tension for a chief who must respond to these influences. A police chief's job security is directly tied to his or her ability to balance these influences against the organization's overall mission.

Police chiefs are in a high-risk profession; secure tenure is far from guaranteed. In many places, the appointing authority has the prerogative to terminate the police chief's employment at any time and for any reason. Although there may be civil service restrictions, or in some states some statutory protection, it is not uncommon for highly respected and competent police chiefs to be fired, or forced to resign, due to circumstances beyond their control. As a chief you no longer have the security you did as a police commander. A chief operates in a volatile and erratic environment where unexpected events and politics can conspire to cost you your job.

What happens when you are forced to leave your job? There are not many options. If you are very lucky, you might find a comparable job in six months, but a year is more the norm. The selection and hiring process for police chiefs can be agonizingly slow. In many instances, police chiefs, after being out of work for months and living on rapidly dwindling savings, find themselves accepting a job that represents a lateral move, or perhaps even a step down. An employment agreement can help mitigate the effect of this potential problem.

In an ideal world, a police chief has an all-inclusive legally binding employment contract that covers all of the conditions of employment. Such a contract would outline all conditions of employment and the salary and benefits package, especially those that go beyond the city's standard benefit package. For example, it would include salary, provisions for annual review and pay increase, househunting trips, moving expense reimbursement, vehicle allowance, lease or use of a car (for personal and business reasons), life insurance, vacation and sick leave, earned vacation and sick leave days, business and civic organization dues, provision for business expense reimbursement, and travel and training expenses. In return, the prospective chief would agree to serve for a fixed period of time, perhaps three to five years, or provide advance notice of resignation (maybe 180 days). However, should the city terminate the contract before the contract's expiration, the chief would receive some type of agreed-upon severance payment. It could range from salary payments for several months up to payments through the end of the contract. Most contracts do allow the city to terminate the contract, without incurring any liability payment, "for cause," which could mean anything from a felony arrest to unacceptable performance. Carefully consider the exact terminology used in any "termination for cause" provision, to ensure it is not worded so loosely that it essentially allows the authority to fire you due to any dissatisfaction. All of these provisions should be discussed and negotiated.

Long-term employment agreements generally must be in writing to be valid. They can take the form of a multipage contract signed by both parties, and perhaps witnessed. A valid contract could also look like a memorandum of understanding or a letter with all of the terms contained in the text. Some employment offer letters even include a signature line for the recipient to acknowledge receipt and acceptance of the terms. Employment agreements can be worth a lot of money over the course of the contract, so it is probably wise to have an attorney experienced with executive contracts review it before signing.

You may find that many cities are cool to the proposition of signing an employment agreement. You might suggest a provision in the employment agreement called a "performance contract." This allows the city to spell out performance goals that the chief will be responsible for meeting, but in return the chief receives a guarantee that he or she will receive substantial advance notice of termination. The governing body may have to authorize the appointing authority by ordinance or resolution to formally establish performance objectives. The contract should include the method and frequency of performance reviews. For example, there may be an annual review at which the appointing authority determines if the chief met the objectives and, if so, the contract may be extended. There are sample employee performance contracts in Appendix G. Any performance contract should be carefully reviewed by qualified legal counsel because the city might assume it can rightly terminate without any penalty if it perceives that some provision of the contract has been violated.

Advantages to Employer and Chief

A contract encourages administrative stability and continuity, which in turn should promote the orderly development of department initiatives. A contract discourages the politically motivated removal of the chief by contentious hiring authorities, so the chief can work with relative job security and develop a long-term view. The employer may find this is a significant inducement when recruiting top talent. It helps to protect against the loss of executive talent, because other potential employers must, first, risk interfering with a valid contract and assuming the resulting liability, and second, be willing to offer at least comparable contract terms. It may save the city the expense of recruiting and relocating another chief. It provides for a professional and orderly termination process, and avoids messy and protracted legal and administrative disputes. Many cities find that signing a contract is just good business practice.

For a chief, a contract underlines his or her worth to the organization and the community. The job security conferred on a police chief through a contract provides him or her more confidence to act with impartiality and independence. The chief can also concentrate on long-term goals. Should the city include performance goals in the contract, the chief has a clear definition of his or her objectives, and a tangible incentive in return for achieving the established goals. Also, busy mayors and city managers sometimes forget what they agreed to when negotiating to hire a chief. Worse yet, they are replaced by someone who was not a party to the original agreement. The letter or contract serves as the record.

Disadvantages to Employer and Chief

There are down sides of a contract for both parties. For the chief, it may mean working under unexpected poor conditions for a period greater than he or she would like. For the appointing authority, it could mean considerable financial loss if a chief falls short of expectations. A contract may be a tough sell to a reluctant council or skeptical public. A contract may also raise expectations of performance, and the chief may lose some flexibility in potential compensation or benefits during the term of the contract.

Another disadvantage to a fixed-term contract is that when the end of the term approaches, considerable public attention is often paid to the city's decision to extend the contract. Political interference can cloud issues surrounding the police department and the chief's tenure. To avoid such public attention, an open-ended contract with no fixed time period may be preferable. The chief may decide to end the employment relationship by giving an agreed-upon notice (perhaps two or three months). The city may also end the employment relationship for any reason, at any time, by providing the chief with a fixed amount of severance pay (perhaps six to 12 months). This way, either party can end the relationship at any time, yet both are protected. You also avoid an unpleasant public battle over whether the chief stays or goes.

11 | Advice from the Pros

PERF'S 1997 SURVEY of appointed police chiefs of the 500 largest city and county police agencies collected data on many subjects. The responses to three of the questions seemed to be of particular relevance to this book. The three questions were: "What advice would you offer an individual who aspires to a chief's position?," "What were the most significant experiences/achievements that prepared you for your present position?" and "What were the personal/professional attributes that led to your hiring as chief in your current jurisdiction? (i.e., What made you the most qualified? What did the hiring authority like about you?)." Some of the responses to each question were chosen for inclusion in this chapter.

What advice would you offer an individual who aspires to a chief's position?

- Be your own person—live or die by what you believe in, not what you think is the "politically correct" answer for the day.

- Work in many assignments. Learn about budgets.

- Prepare for setbacks and failure because success is determined by factors beyond your control. In all cases, personal and professional integrity is paramount.

- Work hard, take care of your people, never be afraid to make the tough decisions and get a good supportive group of peer chiefs to bounce ideas off of. Get an advanced degree and read any law enforcement information you can. Stay ahead of the learning curve regarding technology and trends.

- Know what you are getting into. If you have a strong dedication to the community and don't mind working 80 hours a week and enjoy dealing with the public, media, politicians, unions, and don't mind public criticism and loss of privacy, this can be the most rewarding job of all.

- Get a total understanding of the position, city, community, and the history of the department.

- Work in various assignments within the organization. [Get a] good education. Read everything that comes your way and learn from the mistakes of others.

- Be sure that you are fully prepared to commit your personal energies and time to developing relationships internally and externally. Also be sure your family is willing to accept your commitment to time away from the family.

- Don't bother unless it is a small town with a stable community and department. The years the job will take off of your life is not worth the slightly extra pay and prestige that wears off quickly.

- Recognize it's a very political position and understand the mentality of elected officials and fiscal potential to effect positive changes.

- Start thinking and acting like a chief. The position will come.

- Develop a sense of humor; find several mentors who are successful police chiefs.

- Work, study, do an internship, and find a mentor.

- Learn as much as possible about the political landscape and develop good people skills.

- Watch out for the politics. Don't expect to make everyone happy. You need a strong self image to survive. Never sacrifice your integrity. Find some outside interests away from the job.

- Be prepared, remember the golden rule, always keep your finger on the pulse of the community.

- Remember the following:

  1. You are there to serve your community, not your career.

  2. Stash your ego; admit when you are wrong.

  3. 99.9% of any police organization wants to do the right thing.

  4. Recognize and reward their effort.

  5. If you have to micromanage, then your management and leadership skills need to be examined.

  6. Keep a proper perspective; the sun does not rise or shine on what you do.

  7. Most importantly, have a life, hobbies and other interests.

  8. Family comes first.

- Obtain higher education, work hard, keep abreast of current trends in law enforcement, take nothing for granted, be positive and confident, be goal-oriented.

- Realize that you are part of city government, which means to be successful you must be a team player.

- Get your masters in public administration. Learn about assimilated leadership. Learn as much as you can about egos, politics, and organizational behavior and don't compromise your ethical values for anyone.

- Make sure you can make the tough no-win decisions. Ask yourself if you are the better #2 person than #1. Are you prepared to be fired for doing the right thing?

- Talk to chiefs, especially with long tenure and find out their secrets of success. Also, it's like riding a motorcycle.

Always ride cautious; don't get overly confident and feel you are invulnerable, and when you do take risks, keep the odds on your side and carefully weigh the pros and cons. Stay upright.

- Make sure they understand what they are getting into. Your dream can be a nightmare. Being a captain sure was great.

- Make sure you're eligible for retirement and have a sufficient income available (other than salary).

- Think it over carefully; it is a huge change.

- Maintain relationships in the public (outside of the police department) but stay plugged in to all levels of the department.

- Study the target community (research, research, research). Learn to work with the media and communicate with politicians. Be ready to work long hours if you expect to survive. Make friends with the media. Be open, honest and accessible.

- Become very familiar with the job and your union contract, because current union practices will be your major obstruction regarding your ability to manage and train your human resources.

- Be aware of how alone you really are at the top. Be cognizant of who you can trust when the chips are really down.

- It is the biggest professional challenge you will ever face. The highs are stimulating. The lows are wrenching—just like being in love.

- Remember you are asking for it. No one is forcing you to apply.

- Be prepared for turmoil, be politically astute, morally right and committed to bettering the agency.

- Negotiate a favorable contract and don't overestimate how long you can effectively keep the appointment.

- Develop broad views of policing. Never forget the public perspective. Don't take the job unless you can financially afford to leave it if things are not going well.

- Have a thick skin—you'll receive criticism both internally and externally no matter how good a job you're doing.

- It's not worth dying for. Keep your sense of humor; don't take the problems home.

- Remember it's political not personal. If it's time to leave don't take it personally. If you are not ready to accept the political aspects, don't take the job.

- Understand organizational behavior, do not get alarmed about external and internal criticism, exercise, have a life outside the station.

- Be prepared to work harder and longer than you ever have. Commit to excellence; understand the politics of the position; and build partnerships with your staff, officers, fellow chiefs, department heads, and listen mentally to your customers.

- Do not ever forget what it's like to be a cop.

- Work for your community, not for money. Aspire to be your department and city's police chief, not just a police chief.

- Recognize that tenure is an extremely fragile concept.

- Develop patience in dealing with the various political and community groups that vie for your attention. Any show of frustration is immediately assumed to be a weakness on your part. Learn to communicate with the media at a professional level.

- Get a good education, work your tail off in your current assignments, be accessible to the community so that you'll have their support.

- Have the courage to tell the truth and most importantly be a person of unblemished integrity.

- Develop the ability to effectively delegate.

- Do your homework! Research the community posture, the style of the city manager and administration, the political landscape and above all, where is the union in its political influence with the elected leadership. Get a contract!!

- Continue to be involved, put forth ideas, educate yourself, attend schools, read and keep current on police issues. Above all, do as best as you can in the position you currently hold.

- "Heavy is the head that wears the crown."

- Prepare yourself to have most every decision challenged and second guessed by someone.

- Learn to assimilate into a community as a police chief and a citizen.

- Negotiate a contract if possible and don't let politics guide decisions.

- Practice what you preach! The seeds you sow, so shall you reap! Set the example! Be sincerely committed to your citizens, your employees, and your superiors! Be fair as you can be! There is no right way to do a wrong thing.

- Know your personnel and use them properly. Learn computer use and technology. Keep current.

- Don't take issues too personally. Most things that are of concern on Monday are forgotten by Friday. Make top level personnel selections very carefully; 90% of all of your happiness or all of your misery will come from those selections.

- Understand that many things beyond your control can affect your tenure.

- Be an excellent speaker and be prepared to work twice as many hours as before.

- Develop basic management skills. Volunteer to head a major project from funding to finish. Involve yourself in association committee work.

- Your family will find your position more difficult than you will.

What were the most significant experiences/achievements that prepared you for your present position?

- Promotion through ranks.

- Attending Senior Management Institute for Police and National Academy.

- Reading, college, military combat, current events, compassion of fellowship, work ethics and experience.

- FBI, NA, previous chiefs were excellent teachers, administration experience.

- Northwestern University Traffic Institute, long course.

- Long tenure with varied public assignments and a lot of public exposure.

- Top administrative experience and working close to chiefs in other departments.

- Learn that employees will throw you under the bus to get what they want.

- Prior experience as appointed chief and five years teaching administration part time at the state university.

- Rotation of many jobs in the department gave me a good understanding of a chief's position.

- Being part of an administrative staff for eight years. Headed by a chief who was also a teacher to those around him.

- Twenty-three years of doing my best to be the best. Served in all major divisions of police work.

- Working alongside my predecessor for years and learning from a good man and good administration.

- Working in the city manager's office. Serving twice in interim positions as director or assistant director in other municipal departments. Southwestern Law Enforcement Institute and Command College.

- Administration of a multi-jurisdictional, multi-agency narcotics task force.

- None. There is no comparison between any lower rank and chief.

- Completion of Southern Police Institute and various supervisory experiences in every unit of the department. Completion of the LEEDS.

- The ability to command the community relations bureau division.

- I had excellent mentors.

- FBI Academy, community policing implementation experience.

- Implementing a broad-based community policing program that received widespread acceptance.

- College, Command College, temporary assignment as assistant city manager, temporary assignment as interim chief.

- Ten years as chief in another city.

- Strong combination of field and administrative experience. Three years as a deputy chief. Goal in academic education also helps.

- Varied work experience prior to police work, good moral upbringing by parents, competitive spirit.

- Exposure to every possible police problem or issue—lots of chances to make mistakes.

- Community outreach work taught me to value differences.

- Having served as a second in command in a dynamic police agency.

- People skills.

- Integrity and openness.

- Mobility within the department by taking on new position within two to four years.

- Executive development training, former chief mentoring, being a parent.

- Nine years in the private sector and a broad range of assignments in the department.

- My education and working closely with the police chiefs that preceded me.

- Experience in budgeting, planning, training, labor relations, and internal affairs.

- Eight years as second in command throughout all of the divisions of a large department (and the administrative and leadership changes there) as well as the experience of learning and teaching about the effectiveness of the community policing concept.

- Perseverance, compassion and mentoring with some of the profession's finest.

- The opportunity to work in the major divisions and bureaus of police departments along with community involvement and formal education.

- Executive training (PERF, NOBLE, IACP, Southern Police Institute).

- Working in a department that has little resources and that is underbudgeted provides invaluable experience. It forces creativity, problem solving, building partnerships, figuring out how to get things done in the face of adversity.

- I was relatively unprepared.

- Keeping myself free of apathy and negativity that claimed many others.

- Public speaking training.

- Experience in budgeting.

- Mixing with chiefs at meetings and conferences and learning from their experiences.

- Multiple agency experience.

- Twenty years in same organization and community.

- Common sense, compassion and a sense of humor given to me by my parents.

- Held a supervisory staff position, was heavily involved in policy making and the budget process for a full seven years prior to making chief.

- Prior command-level experience in larger agency, SPI, accreditation manager, involvement in community policing at prior agency.

- Schools, lectures by chiefs, programs presented by chiefs at regional and national meetings.

- Working directly as an executive officer for five different chiefs.

- Participating in athletics taught me perseverance and resiliency. Also experience and education taught me decision making.

- Length of service in diverse management positions, college education, SMIP attendance. Not being just an administrator, leadership, and principles.

- Addressing public on conflicting issues.

- My five years experience as an assistant chief were very helpful.

- I was born in and still live in the community, elevated through the ranks and served in every bureau. Also served on boards on both police unions, have good understanding of rank and file concerns, and community concerns.

- Active participation in professional organizations.

What were the personal/professional attributes that led to your hiring as chief in your current jurisdiction? (i.e., What made you the most qualified? What did the hiring authority like about you?)

- Internal support from the department. Standing reputation from the community.

- Work experience, organizational skills, and community-oriented policing experience.

- Experience as a change agent, familiar with the community.

- Success in prior organizations.

- Education, experience and community involvement.

- My policing experience, my philosophy and my personality matched the community.

- Reputation, experience and training.

- Chemistry between city council. As a native of state, more likely to integrate into the community. Professional qualifications.

- Attitude, education, experience and ability.

- Retired from a large multi-ethnic city with much experience. Proven record to be a change agent.

- I got along well with the city people and I was going to bring about change in the department.

- Knowledge and commitment to community policing, fairness, integrity and the ability to achieve results. Knowledge of community.

- My two years as deputy chief with the same department.

- Knowledge of department will make you well respected internally and externally; plan for implementing community policing.

- Commitment, integrity, people skills, stability, and visionary.

- Master's degree, leadership skills, integrity, work ethic.

- Education, experience as chief, interpersonal skills, new innovative programs.

- Education, professional experience, reputation for integrity, community policing background.

- Honest, open, direct. Works well with city staff. Supported by the community and police union.

- Political neutrality; other candidates had strong political ties.

- Combination of experience and documented successes that fit the community program.

- Collaborative, approachable, respected, integrity, and experience.

- Diverse résumé with aspects of all commands in community policing. People person, social style.

- Background with diverse culture, strong management skills, potential for long-term stability.

- Prior experience as an accreditation manager, and two MBA degrees.

- Open communication style, knowledge of community willingness to make changes.

- Good chemistry with the county's expectations, education, experience and reputation.

- Collaborative management style, track record in making programs work.

- Varied background, young with new ideas, good chemistry with management and panel.

- Vast experience within the department. Advanced education and previous success.

- Community support.

- Performance in assessment exercises.

- City council support.

- Experience in like situation.

- Leadership skills, community policing experience, public speaking ability.

- Positive reputation, inside the organization and within the community. Quality leadership credibility, knowledge of the organization and an understanding of the community and organizational issues.

- Education level, multiple graduate degrees, experience teaching at a college level, prior internal affairs experience.

- Tenure, reputation, recommendation to manager from peer about abilities.

- Experience, professionalism, communications ability, reputation for innovation, creativity, integrity, commitment to community policing and excellence.

- Education, experience, extensive budget and operational experience; ability to work with elected officials; creativity and innovation.

- Integrity, energy level, communication skills.

- Prior experience as a chief of police.

- Common sense approach to community policing.

- Vast experience in other agencies.

- Skills gained from position in much larger department.

- Articulation of the need to radically change our traditional approach to policing to one oriented to community partnership and problem resolution.

- Successful law enforcement career, communication skills, education, biracial support.

- Community policing philosophy, openness on diversity, respect of rank and file and community.

- My high profile support from community involvement in policing.

- Experience with and perceived ability to implement community policing as new chief, overall experience and performance in assessment center, communication skills.

- Community policing background, fit with police and city organization.

- Outstanding educational and professional background, chemistry between manager and me was right.

- Provided the qualities that the city manager wanted and needed. Stable and internal support; my department is in synchronization with other departments within the city.

- Senior rank, educational credentials, experience, life-long city resident.

Appendices

State Leagues of Cities

Alabama League of Cities
P.O. Box 1270
Montgomery, Alabama 36102
(334) 262-2566

Alaska Municipal League
207 Second St., Suite 200
Juneau, Alaska 99801
(907) 586-1325

**League of Arizona Cities
and Towns**
1820 West Washington St.
Phoenix, Arizona 85007
(602) 258-5786

Arkansas Municipal League
301 W. Second St.
North Little Rock, Arkansas 72115
(501) 374-4638

League of California Cities
1400 K St., 4th Floor
Sacramento, California 95814
(916) 658-8200

Colorado Municipal League
1144 Sherman St.
Denver, Colorado 80203
(303) 831-6411

**Connecticut Conference
of Municipalities**
900 Chapel St., 9th Floor
New Haven, Connecticut 06510
(203) 498-3000

**Delaware League of
Local Governments**
134 E. Water St.
Dover, Delaware 19903
(302) 678-0991

Florida League of Cities
301 S. Bronough
Tallahassee, Florida 32301
(904) 222-9684

Georgia Municipal Association
201 Pryor St., SW
Atlanta, Georgia 30303
(404) 688-0472

Association of Idaho Cities
3314 Grace St.
Boise, Idaho 83703
(208) 344-8594

Illinois Municipal League
500 E. Capitol Ave.
Springfield, Illinois 62701
(217) 525-1220

**Indiana Association of
Cities and Towns**
150 West Market St., Suite 728
Indianapolis, Indiana 46204
(317) 237-6200

Iowa League of Cities
317 Sixth Ave., Suite 1400
Des Moines, Iowa 50309
(515) 244-7282

League of Kansas Municipalities
300 SW 8th St.
Topeka, Kansas 66603
(785) 354-9565

Kentucky League of Cities, Inc.
101 East Vine St., Suite 600
Lexington, Kentucky 40507
(606) 323-3700

Louisiana Municipal Association
700 N. 10th St.
Baton Rouge, Louisiana 70802
(504) 344-5001

Maine Municipal Association
60 Community Drive
Augusta, Maine 04330
(207) 623-8428

Maryland Municipal League
1212 West St.
Annapolis, Maryland 21401
(301) 268-5514

Massachusetts Municipal Association
60 Temple Place, 2nd Floor
Boston, Massachusetts 02111
(617) 426-7272

Michigan Municipal League
1675 Green Road
Ann Arbor, Michigan 48106
(734) 662-3246

League of Minnesota Cities
145 University Ave. West
St. Paul, Minnesota 55103
(651) 281-1200

Mississippi Municipal Association
600 East Amite St., Suite 104
Jackson, Mississippi 39201
(601) 353-5854

Missouri Municipal League
1727 Southridge Drive
Jefferson City, Missouri 65109
(314) 635-9134

Montana League of Cities and Towns
208 N. Montana, Capital 1 Center
Helena, Montana 59601
(406) 442-8768

League of Nebraska Municipalities
1335 L St.
Lincoln, Nebraska 68508
(402) 476-2829

Nevada League of Cities
206 N. Carson
Carson City, Nevada 89701
(702) 882-2121

New Hampshire Municipal Association
25 Triangle Park Drive
Concord, New Hampshire 03301
(603) 224-7447

New Jersey State League of Municipalities
407 West State St.
Trenton, New Jersey 08618
(609) 695-3481

New Mexico Municipal League
1229 Paseo de Peralta
Santa Fe, New Mexico 87504
(505) 982-5573

New York State Conference of Mayors and Municipal Officials
119 Washington Ave.
Albany, New York 12210
(518) 463-1185

**North Carolina League
of Municipalities**
215 N. Dawson
Raleigh, North Carolina 27602
(919) 715-4000

North Dakota League of Cities
1710 Burnt Boat Drive
Bismarck, North Dakota 58501
(701) 223-3518

Ohio Municipal League
175 South Third St., Suite 510
Columbus, Ohio 43215
(614) 221-4349

Oklahoma Municipal League
201 N.E. 23rd St.
Oklahoma City, Oklahoma 73105
(405) 528-7515

League of Oregon Cities
1201 Court St. NE
Salem, Oregon 97301
(503) 588-6550

**Pennsylvania League of
Cities and Municipalities**
414 N. Second St.
Harrisburg, Pennsylvania 17101
(717) 236-9469

**Rhode Island League of
Cities and Towns**
1 State St., Suite 502
Providence, Rhode Island 02908
(401) 272-3434

**Municipal Association of
South Carolina**
1529 Washington St.
Columbia, South Carolina 29211
(803) 799-9574

South Dakota Municipal League
214 East Capitol
Pierre, South Dakota 57501
(605) 224-8654

Tennessee Municipal League
226 Capitol Blvd., Room 710
Nashville, Tennessee 37219
(615) 255-6416

Texas Municipal League
1821 Rutherford Lane, Suite 400
Austin, Texas 78754
(512) 719-6300

Utah League of Cities and Towns
50 South 600 East, Suite 150
Salt Lake City, Utah 84102
(801) 328-1601

**Vermont League of
Cities and Towns**
89 Main St., Suite 4
Montpelier, Vermont 05602
(802) 229-9111

Virginia Municipal League
13 East Franklin St.
Richmond, Virginia 23219
(804) 649-8471

Association of Washington Cities
1076 South Franklin St.
Olympia, Washington 98501
(360) 753-4137

West Virginia Municipal League
2020 Kanawha Blvd. East
Charleston, West Virginia 25311
(304) 342-5564

League of Wisconsin Municipalities
202 State St., Suite 300
Madison, Wisconsin 53703
(608) 267-2380

**Wyoming Association of
Municipalities**
200 East 8th Ave.
Cheyenne, Wyoming 82001
(307) 632-0398

B | State and Regional Police Chief Associations

Alabama
Executive Director
Alabama Association of Chiefs of Police
P.O. Box 341
Brewton, AL 36427
334-867-4605
Fax: 334-867-5531

Alaska
President
Alaska Association of Chiefs of Police
Chief Duane S. Udland
Anchorage Police Department
4501 S. Bragaw St.
Anchorage, AK 99507-1599
907-786-8590
Fax: 907-786-8638

Arizona
Executive Director
Arizona Association of Chiefs of Police
P.O. Box 6638
Phoenix, AZ 85005
602-223-2861
Fax: 602-223-2917

Arkansas
Executive Director
Arkansas Association of Chiefs of Police
P.O. Box 94375
North Little Rock, AR 72190-4375
501-753-5611
Fax: 501-753-5919

California
Executive Director
California Police Chiefs Association
1455 Response Road, Suite 190
Sacramento, CA 95815
916-923-0545
Fax: 916-263-6090

Colorado
Executive Director
Colorado Association of
Chiefs of Police
2701 Alcott St., #386
Denver, CO 80211
303-480-1247
Fax: 303-458-1213

Connecticut
Executive Director
Connecticut Police Chiefs Association
342 N. Main St.
West Hartford, CT 06117-2507
860-586-7506
Fax: 860-586-7550

Delaware
Delaware Police Chiefs Council
Chairman
Chief Keith I. Faulkner
Dover Police Department
400 S. Queen Street
Dover, DE 19904
302-736-7101
Fax: 302-736-7146

Florida
Executive Director
Florida Police Chiefs Association
P.O. Box 14038
Tallahassee, FL 32317-4038
904-385-9046
Fax: 904-386-3272

Georgia
Executive Director
Georgia Association of Chiefs of Police
P.O. Box 450921
Atlanta, GA 31145
770-414-6494
Fax: 770-414-6496
E-mail: gacp@mindspring.com

Hawaii
Hawaii State Law Enforcement
Officials Association
President/Representative
Chief Lee Donohue
Honolulu Police Department
801 S. Beretania St.
Honolulu, HI 96813-2920
808-529-3162
Fax: 808-529-3030

Idaho
President
Idaho Chiefs of Police Association
Chief William Gordon
Meridian Police Department
201 E. Idaho
Meridian, ID 83642
208-888-6678
Fax: 208-884-5077

Illinois
Executive Director
Illinois Association of Chiefs of Police
426 S. Fifth Street, Suite 200
Springfield, IL 62701
217-523-3765
Fax: 217-523-8352
E-mail: gkoertge@ilchiefs.org

Indiana
Executive Director
Indiana Association of Chiefs of Police
10293 N. Meridian St., Suite 175
Indianapolis, IN 46290
317-816-1619
Fax: 317-816-1633
E-mail: mfw@wardmanage.com

Iowa
Iowa Police Executive Forum
President
Chief Jeffrey R. Cayler
Carroll Police Department
112 E. 5th St.
Carroll, IA 51401
712-792-3536
Fax: 712-792-1310

Kansas
Executive Director
Kansas Association of Chiefs of Police
P.O. Box 780603
Wichita, KS 67278-0603
316/733-7300
Fax 316/733-7301

Kentucky
Executive Director
Kentucky Association of
Chiefs of Police
Eastern Kentucky University
467 Stratton
Richmond, KY 40475
606-622-6187
Fax: 606-622-6606
E-mail: craigbird@aol.com

Louisiana
Executive Director
Louisiana Association of
Chiefs of Police
603 Europe St.
Baton Rouge, LA 70802
504-387-3261
Fax: 504-387-3262

Maine
Executive Director
Maine Chiefs of Police Association
93 Silver St.
Waterville, ME 04901
207-873-0455
Fax: 207-767-2214

Maryland
Executive Administration Officer
Morris Lewis
Maryland Chiefs of Police Association
P.O. Box 4686
Largo, MD 20775
301-218-1745
Fax: 301-218-1746
E-mail: mdchiefs@aol.com or
         mlewis6306@aol.com

Massachusetts
Executive Director
Massachusetts Chiefs of
Police Association
47 Memorial Drive
Shrewsbury, MA 01545-4028
508-842-1556
Fax: 508-842-3703

Michigan
Executive Director
Michigan Association of
Chiefs of Police
2133 University Park Drive, #200
Okemos, MI 48864-3975
517-349-9420
Fax: 517-349-5823

Minnesota
Executive Director
Minnesota Chiefs of Police Association
1220 S. Concord
South St. Paul, MN 55075
612-457-0677
Fax: 612-457-5665

Mississippi
Mississippi Association of
Chiefs of Police
President
Chief Bill Ladd
West Point Police Department
P.O. Box 1117
West Point, MS 39773
601-494-1244
Fax: 601-494-1398

Missouri
Executive Director
Missouri Police Chiefs Association
600 E. Capitol Ave.
Jefferson City, MO 65101
800-264-6472
573-636-5444
Fax: 573-636-6634

Montana
Montana Association of Chiefs of Police
President/Representative
Chief Pete Lawrenson
Missoula Police Department
435 Ryman
Missoula, MT 59802-4297
406-523-4682
Fax: 406-728-6690

Nebraska
Police Chiefs Association of Nebraska
President
Chief Melvin Griggs
Gering Police Department
1025 P St.
Gering, NE 69341
308-436-5089
Fax: 308-436-6898

Nevada
Nevada Sheriffs and Chiefs Association
President
Chief David Mullin
Boulder City Police Department
P.O. Box 61350
Boulder City, NV 89006-1350
702-293-9224
Fax: 702-293-9224

**New England Association of
Chiefs of Police**
Executive Director
North Attleboro Police Department
16 Mason Ave.
North Attleboro, MA 02760
508-695-1212
Fax: 508-695-2162

New Hampshire
New Hampshire Association of
Chiefs of Police
President
Chief Russell E. Lary
Grantham Police Department
P.O. Box 704
Grantham, NH 03753-0704
603-863-6844
Fax: 603-863-8152

New Jersey
Executive Director
New Jersey Association of
Chiefs of Police
777 Alexander Road, Suite 203
Princeton, NJ 08540
609-452-0014
Fax: 609-452-1893

New Mexico
New Mexico Association of
Chiefs of Police President
Chief Richard Melton
Los Alamos Police Department
2500 Trinity Drive
Los Alamos, NM 87544
505-662-8226
Fax: 505-662-8287

New York
Executive Director
New York State Association of
Chiefs of Police
2697 Hamburg St.
Schenectady, NY 12303
518-355-3371
Fax: 518-356-5767
E-mail: NYSCOP@CITYUSA.NET

North Carolina
Executive Director
North Carolina Association of
Chiefs of Police
P.O. Box 1589
Raleigh, NC 27602
919-829-9119
Fax: 919-833-1959

North Dakota
North Dakota Association of
Chiefs of Police
President
Chief Dave Miller
Casselton Police Department
701 First St. N.
Casselton, ND 58012
701-347-4861
Fax: 701-347-4505

Ohio
Executive Director
Ohio Association of Chiefs of Police, Inc.
6277 Riverside Drive, #2N
Dublin, OH 43017-5067
614-761-0330
Fax: 614-718-3216
E-mail: wursch@oacp.org

Oklahoma
Executive Director
Oklahoma Association of
Chiefs of Police
3701 S.E. 15th St., Suite 100
Del City, OK 73115
888-528-6227
405-672-1225
Fax: 405-670-8763
E-mail: Staceyoacp@juno.com

Oregon
Executive Staff
Oregon Association of Chiefs of Police
727 Center St., N.E., Suite 300
Salem, OR 97301
503-315-1411
Fax: 503-315-1416

Pennsylvania
Executive Director
Pennsylvania Chiefs of
Police Association
2941 N. Front St.
Harrisburg, PA 17110
717-236-1059
Fax: 717-236-0226

Rhode Island
Rhode Island Police Chiefs Association
President
Chief William McCombe
New Shoreham Police Department
P.O. Box 307
Block Island, RI 02807
401-466-3220
Fax: 401-466-3228

South Carolina
Executive Director
South Carolina Police Chiefs Association
P.O. Box 61170
Columbia, SC 29260-1170
803-738-1879

South Dakota
Executive Director
South Dakota Police Chiefs Association
214 E. Capitol
Pierre, SD 57501
605-224-8654
Fax: 605-224-8655

Tennessee
Executive Secretary
Tennessee Association of
Chiefs of Police
P.O. Box 498
Chapel Hill, TN 37034
931-364-2326
Fax: 931-364-2588

Texas
Executive Director
Texas Police Chiefs Association
P.O. Box 81095
Austin, TX 78708-1095
512-869-8372
Fax: 512-863-6653

Utah
Executive Director
Utah Association of Chiefs of Police
3135 South 3600 West
West Valley, UT 84119
801-254-0313
Fax: 801-254-3479

Vermont
Chiefs of Police Association of Vermont
President
Chief Michael McCarthy
Swanton Police Department
120 First St.
Swanton, VT 05488
802-868-4100
Fax: 802-868-3930
E-mail: ChiefMac@cji.net

Virginia
Executive Director
Virginia Association of Chiefs of Police
8003 Franklin Farms Drive, Suite 111
Richmond, VA 23288
804-285-8227
Fax: 804-285-3363
E-mail: vachiefs@aol.com

Washington
Executive Director
Washington Association of
Sheriffs and Police Chiefs
P.O. Box 826
Olympia, WA 98507
360-586-3221
Fax: 360-586-7030
E-mail: larrye@thurston.com

West Virginia
West Virginia Chiefs of
Police Association
President
Chief Carl Kocher
New Martinsville Police Department
193 Main St.
New Martinsville, WV 26155
304-455-9100
Fax: 304-455-9102

Wisconsin
Executive Secretary
Wisconsin Chiefs of Police, Inc.
116 Humphrey Circle South
Shawano, WI 54166
715-524-8283
Fax: 715-524-8280
E-mail: dthaves@frontiernet.net

Wyoming
Executive Director
Wyoming Sheriffs and
Police Chiefs Association
8817 Sherman Mountain Road
Cheyenne, WY 82009
307-632-9187
Fax: 307-637-0025

Source: *Membership Directory, February 1999,* International Association of Chiefs of Police, Division of State Associations of Chiefs of Police.

C Resources for Professional Information, Membership and Police Chief Advertising

Professional Organizations

Academy of Criminal Justice Sciences
1500 N. Beauregard St., #101
Alexandria, VA 22311
800-757-ACJS
703-379-2090
Fax: 703-379-8867
www.acjs.org
Publishes *ACJS Today* four times a year and, along with the Police Executive Research Forum, publishes *Police Quarterly*.

American Correctional Association
4380 Forbes Blvd.
Lanham, MD 20706
800-222-5646
301-918-1800
Fax: 301-918-1900
www.corrections.com/aca

American Society of Criminology
1314 Kinnear Road, #214
Columbus, OH 43212
614-292-9207
Fax: 614-292-6767
www.asc41.com
Publishes *Criminologist* bimonthly and *Criminology* quarterly.

Commission of Accreditation for Law Enforcement Agencies, Inc. (CALEA)
10306 Eaton Place
Suite 320
Fairfax, VA 22030
800-368-3757
Fax: 703-591-2206
www.calea.org

Community Policing Consortium
1726 M Street, NW
Suite 801
Washington, DC 20036
800-833-3085
202-833-3305
Fax: 202-833-9295
www.communitypolicing.org

Hispanic American Police Command Officer Association (HAPCOA)
6801 Coolridge Road
Camp Springs, MD 20748-2705
301-449-7967
Fax: 301-449-7077
www.hapcoa.org
Publishes newsletter and distributes information to membership via a fax network.

International Association of Campus Law Enforcement Administrators (IACLEA)
342 North Main St.
West Hartford, CT 06117
860-586-7517
Fax: 860-586-7550
www.iaclea.org
Bimonthly membership journal, *The Campus Law Enforcement Journal,* and web site list positions.

International Association of Chiefs of Police (IACP)
515 N. Washington St.
Alexandria, VA 22314
800-843-4227
Fax: 703-836-4543
www.theiacp.org
Publishes *Police Chief* magazine monthly, which is a major source of nationally advertised positions.

International Association of Women Police (IAWP)
5423 W. Sunnyside Ave.
Chicago, IL 60630
773-736-3405
www.iawp.org
Publishes a quarterly magazine, *Women Police.*

International City/County Management Association (ICMA)
777 North Capitol St. NE
Suite 500
Washington, DC 20002
202-289-4262
Fax: 202-962-3500
www.icma.com
Publishes monthly magazine, *Public Administration,* and a job announcement newsletter called *J.O.B. (Job Opportunities Bulletin).*

National Association of Women Law Enforcement Executives (NAWLEE)
Chief Diane M. Skoog
Carver Police Department
3 Dunham St.
Carver, MA 02330
508-666-2000
www.nawlee.com
Publishes quarterly newsletter, *NAWLEE News.* Has a listserve for members that provides job announcements.

National League of Cities
1301 Pennsylvania Ave. NW
6th Floor
Washington, DC 20004
202-626-3000
Fax: 202-626-3043
www.nlc.org
Publishes *Nations's Cities Weekly,* which may include vacancies.

National Organization of Black Law Enforcement Executives (NOBLE)
4609 Pinecrest Office Park Drive, Suite F
Alexandria, VA 22312
703-658-1529
Fax: 703-658-9479
www.noblenatl.org
Publishes a monthly newsletter and magazine approximately three times per year. They also have a job line listing positions (301-352-0842 option 6).

Police Executive Research Forum (PERF)
1120 Connecticut Ave. NW, Suite 930
Washington, DC 20036
202-466-7820
Fax: 202-466-7826
www.PoliceForum.org
Publishes monthly newsletter, *Subject to Debate,* with employment listings, as well as postings on PERF's web site.

National Criminal Justice Association
444 N. Capitol St. NW, Suite 618
Washington, DC 20001
202-624-1440
Fax: 202-508-3859
www.sso.org/ncja

National District Attorneys Association
99 Canal Center Plaza, Suite 510
Alexandria, VA 22314
703-549-9222
Fax: 703-836-3195
www.ndaa-apri.org

National Sheriffs' Association
1450 Duke St.
Alexandria, VA 22314
703-836-7827
Fax: 703-683-6541
www.sheriffs.org

Police Foundation
1001 Connecticut Ave. NW
Suite 200
Washington, DC 20037
202-833-1460
Fax: 202-659-9149
www.policefoundation.org

U.S. Conference of Mayors
1620 Eye St. NW
Washington, DC 20006
202-293-7330
Fax: 202-293-2352
www.usmayors.org
Publishes a bimonthly journal for members.

Other Periodicals

The Chronicle of Higher Education
1255 23rd St. NW, Suite 700
Washington, DC 20037-1190
202-466-1000
Fax: 202-452-1033
Weekly newspaper that lists campus law enforcement openings.

Crime Control Digest
3702 Pender Drive
Suite 300
Fairfax, VA 22030
800-422-9267
703-352-4811
Fax: 703-352-2323
Crime Control Digest is published weekly, *Community Policing Digest* is published semimonthly.

Criminal Justice Newsletter
1900 L St., Suite 312
Washington, D.C. 20036
202-835-1770
Fax: 202-835-1772
Bimonthly newsletter lists job announcements.

Law Enforcement News
John Jay College of Criminal Justice
City University of New York
899 Tenth Ave.
New York, NY 10019
212-237-8442
Fax: 212-237-8486
Law Enforcement News (LEN) is published approximately biweekly, and includes occasional job announcements. Additionally, a regular feature called People & Places frequently mentions retirements and hirings of police chiefs.

Law & Order
1000 Skokie Blvd., Suite 500
Wilmette, IL 60091
847-256-8555
Fax: 847-256-8574
Monthly magazine lists some advertisements and classified ads for vacancies.

Government Agencies

Bureau of Justice Assistance
U.S. Department of Justice
810 7th St., NW
Washington, DC 20531
202-514-6278
www.ojp.usdoj.gov/BJA

Bureau of Justice Statistics
U.S. Department of Justice
810 7th St., NW
Washington, DC 20531
202-307-0765
www.ojp.usdoj.gov/bjs/

National Criminal Justice Reference Service (NCJRS)
P. O. Box 6000
Rockville, MD 20849-6000
800-851-3420
askncjrs@ncjrs.org
puborders@ncjrs.org

Office of Community Oriented Policing Services
U.S. Department of Justice
1100 Vermont Ave.
10th Floor
Washington, DC 20005
202-616-2888
Fax: 202-616-2914
www.usdoj.gov/cops

National Institute of Justice
U.S. Department of Justice
801 7th St., NW
Washington, DC 20531
202-307-2942
Fax: 202-307-6394
www.ojp.usdoj.gov/nij

Other Internet Resources

www.govtjobs.com/safe
Lists public safety job vacancies.

www.govtjob.net
Local government job net offers publications and software.

www.policechief.com
Lists information about police chief vacancies.

www.careerpath.com
Career management site for job seekers and employers. Also offers tools for career management.

www.careerbuilder.com
Offers advice on finding a job and tips for getting hired.

www.ajb.dni.us
America's Job Bank (sponsored by the U.S. Department of Labor and various state public employment services).

www.newspapers.com
Newspapers from around the country can be accessed from this web site.

www.newslink.org
Links to newspapers, magazines, broadcasters and news services.

www.census.gov
This is the U.S. Census web site, providing useful information on communities.

APPENDIX C

Executive Search Firms

Bennett Associates

Richard T. Bennett, Principal
335 Washington St., Suite 12
Norwell, MA 02061
781-659-9950 ext. 12
Fax: 781-659-9969

The Brimeyer Group, Inc.

Jim Brimeyer, President
904 Main St., Suite 205
Hopkins, MN 55343
612-945-0246
Fax: 612-945-0102
E-mail: brimgroup@aol.com

DMG Maximus

Bob Murray, Vice President
4320 Auburn Blvd., Suite 2000
Sacramento, CA 95841
916-485-8102
Fax: 916-485-0111
E-mail: recruit@dmg.maxinc.com
www.dmgriffith.com

Mike Casey,
Director of Executive Recruiting
630 Dundee Road, Suite 200
Northbrook, IL 60062
847-564-9270
Fax: 847-559-8323
E-mail:
mikecasey@dmg.maxinc.com

Norman Roberts, Vice President
1800 Century Park East, Suite 430
Los Angeles, CA 90067-1507
310-552-1112
Fax: 310-552-1113
E-mail: searchla@dmg.maxinc.com

Hughes, Perry & Associates

Richard Perry, Senior Vice President
Richard Hughes, Senior Vice President
P.O. Box 384
Sea Ranch, CA 95497
707-785-3083
707-785-3086 fax
E-mail: hpa@mcn.org

International Association of Chiefs of Police

Kim Kohlhepp, Manager
Center for Testing and
Executive Search
515 North Washington St.
Alexandria, VA 22314
703-836-6767
Fax: 703-836-4543
E-mail: kohlheppk@theiacp.org
www.theiacp.org

Oldani Group

Jerrold Oldani, President
188 106th Ave. Northeast, Suite 420
Bellevue, WA 98004
425-451-3938
Fax: 425-453-6786
E-mail: searches@theoldanigroup.com
www.theoldanigroup.com

The PAR Group

Paul A. Reaume, President
100 North Waukegan Road, Suite 200
Lake Bluff, IL 60044
847-234-0005
Fax: 847-234-8309
E-mail: pargroup@interaccess.com

Police Executive Research Forum

Chuck Wexler, Executive Director
1120 Connecticut Ave. NW, Suite 930
Washington, DC 20036
202-466-7820
Fax: 202-466-7826
E-mail: perf@PoliceForum.org
www.PoliceForum.org

Police Foundation

Hubert Williams, President
1201 Connecticut Ave. NW, Suite 200
Washington, DC 20036
202-833-1460
Fax: 202-659-9149
E-mail: pfinfo@policefoundation.org

Ralph Andersen & Associates

Heather Renschler,
Senior Vice President
4240 Rocklin Road, Suite 11
Rocklin, CA 95677
916-630-4900
Fax: 916-630-4911
E-mail: raa-hr@pacbell.net
www.ralphanderson.com

Chuck Rohre, Vice President
3920 Black Gold Drive, Suite 202
Dallas, TX 75247
214-956-7097
Fax: 214-351-4471
E-mail: raa@ralphanderson.com

Shannon Associates

John Shannon, CEO
1601 Response Road, Suite 390
Sacramento, CA 95815
916-567-4280
Fax: 916-567-1220
E-mail: resumes@shannonassoc.com

Slavin Management Consultants, Inc.

Robert E. Slavin, President
3040 Holcomb Bridge Road, Suite B-1
Norcross, GA 30071
770-449-4656
Fax: 770-416-0848
E-mail: rslavin101@aol.com

The Mercer Group, Inc.

James L. Mercer, President
5579B Chamblee Dunwoody Road,
Suite 511
Atlanta, GA 30338
770-551-0403
Fax: 770-399-9749
E-mail: mercer@mindspring.com
www.mercergroup.inc.com

Waldron & Company

Fred Pabst
101 Stewart, Suite 101
Seattle, WA 98101
206-441-4144
Fax: 206-441-5213
E-mail: waldronco@aol.com
www.waldron-mpi.com

E Sample Cover Letters

[ADDRESS]
[DATE]

[NAME]
[TITLE]
[ADDRESS]

Dear [NAME]:

In response to your search for a qualified candidate for the position of police chief, City of [CITY], [STATE], I have enclosed my résumé for your consideration. As the first director of public safety for the [AGENCY], I have developed and am implementing a comprehensive safety plan for the [CITY] residents. I am accomplishing this plan through a community-oriented approach to service delivery and a strong collaborative relationship with community stakeholders.

Before this appointment in [DATE], I served for [X] years as a member of the [CITY] Police Department. I retired as commander of the Fourth Police Precinct— the largest, most populous and culturally diverse of the city's 10 police districts. My resource allocation plan, utilizing beat profiling, need-based scheduling and fixed permanent shifts, became a model adopted by the entire police department. As precinct commander, I initiated many other positive programs designed to maximize usage of police resources, while dramatically improving police services. The centerpiece of these initiatives was ensuring that both residents and businesses enjoyed a heightened sense of police involvement. Central to our many successes was our strong belief in, and commitment to, Community Empowerment Policing. I am fully prepared to seek out all available resources and implement collaborative efforts designed to address both crime and quality of life concerns.

In addition to my professional experience, my educational achievements include completion of a master's degree in business administration and the FBI's National Academy.

If I were to serve as the police chief, I would bring to the team a proven track record and a clear understanding of [CITY]'s law enforcement vision.

Sincerely,

[NAME]

[NAME]
[ADDRESS]

[DATE]

[NAME]
[TITLE]
[ADDRESS]

Dear [NAME]:

Thank you for the opportunity to apply for the position of police chief for the [AGENCY]. Enclosed is my résumé, which indicates that my background, experience and education have prepared me for this position. I have also included a list of references, whom you may contact.

The [AGENCY], where I am currently employed, is a full-service police agency of nearly 1,000 employees serving a diverse community of approximately 500,000 citizens. As a district commander serving 200,000 citizens in a 40-square-mile area, I have turned an organization of nearly 200 employees into the premier patrol district in [AGENCY]. Focusing on internal issues has restored the employees' self-esteem and has sparked their renewed interest in innovative policing and improving the quality of life for the citizens we serve.

The partnerships we have forged with the community and other local law enforcement agencies, as well as the creative crime strategies we have put in place, have made our district a model for our police department. We are continuously praised by our police chief for the positive difference we have made through the reduction of violent crime, for our innovative programs, for the confidence that the community has in us, for our employees' enthusiasm and professionalism, and for consistently "getting the job done."

My educational background largely contributed to the successes I have experienced in my current assignment. I earned a bachelor's degree in police science at the [UNIVERSITY]. I graduated from the [UNIVERSITY] criminal justice program with a master's degree in administration. I have continued my education throughout my career, seeking every opportunity to better myself as a police leader. I attended the F.B.I. National Academy and recently graduated from an intense training for new police chiefs. I have been an instructor for the past 16 years, specializing the last 10 in leadership training. I have been a guest lecturer at [UNIVERSITY], and am an adjunct faculty member at our local community college. I am an experienced public speaker, skilled at dealing effectively with diverse groups. I would welcome the opportunity to use my experience and leadership abilities in the [AGENCY].

Sincerely,

[CANDIDATE]

F | Sample Résumés

Teresa C. Chambers
Résumé Highlights

Education:

- Master's degree from The Johns Hopkins University.
- Bachelor's degree from the University of Maryland—University College.
- F.B.I. National Academy, 191st session.
- Chiefs Program, a basic training curriculum for police chiefs.
- Leadership Prince George's, a year-long leadership program.
- More than 50 courses and seminars in law enforcement, supervision, leadership and related skills.

Current Position: District commander, holding the rank of major, in the Prince George's County Police Department, a 1,500+ person police department serving a population of nearly 800,000 citizens in a 488-square-mile urban/rural county bordering Washington, DC. Assigned district is the most diverse within Prince George's County and is home for approximately 200,000 citizens.

Command Experience: Command officer since 1987; experience includes a variety of administrative and operational assignments; rose steadily through the ranks to current rank and assignment.

Related Experience: Consultant for on-site management studies of seven law enforcement agencies across the United States.

Speaking Experience: Experienced, confident public speaker; skilled at dealing effectively with diverse groups.

Certified instructor for more than sixteen years, specializing the past eleven years in leadership training; audiences have included local law enforcement officers and students at Johns Hopkins University, American University, the University of Maryland and the Prince George's County Community College.

Community Involvement: Active participant in community and civic affairs.

Awards and Recognition: Human Relations Award from the National Conference of Christians and Jews and an Outstanding Young Marylander award from the Prince George's Jaycees.

Featured in history book titled *Women of Achievement in Prince George's County History* as well as two local publications, *Women's Issues and Concerns* and the *Prince George's Sentinel*.

One hundred fifty-seven letters of commendation or appreciation.

TERESA C. CHAMBERS
[Home Address]
[Home Phone]
[Work Phone]

FORMAL EDUCATION

The Johns Hopkins University, Baltimore, Maryland.
Master's degree in applied behavioral science
with a concentration in community development, 5-97.
Graduated Summa Cum Laude. GPA: 4.0

University of Maryland University College,
College Park, Maryland.
Bachelor of science in law enforcement, 12-87.
Minor: Health/History.
Graduated Cum Laude. GPA: 3.777

ADDITIONAL TRAINING

F.B.I. National Academy.
191st Session; September 28, 1997, through December 12, 1997.

Chiefs Program, Maryland Police Training Commission.
Graduated in 1996 from a "basic training" program for new police chiefs and prospective chiefs.

Leadership Prince George's, Class IX.
Similar to many of the approximately 800 community leadership programs across the country, this 10-month program (September 1993 through June 1994) enhances leadership skills and cultural flexibility, creates a networking system among community leaders, and engages participants in community issues.

North Florida Institute of Police Technology and Management.
Trained and certified as a traffic accident reconstructionist through six weeks of training between 1983 and 1986.

Maryland Police Training Commission.
Trained and certified in 1982 as an instructor in general police topics and firearms; have maintained certification through present time.

Prince George's County Police Academy.
Graduated December 5, 1978.

Miscellaneous
More than 50 courses and seminars regarding law enforcement, supervision, management, leadership and related topics.

EMPLOYMENT HISTORY

Prince George's County Police Department
1976 to Present
Work as one of the top command officers in the Prince George's County Police Department, a full-service law enforcement agency. Bordering the southeast side of Washington, DC, Prince George's County is home for nearly 800,000 individuals. Its rich diversity and progressive police department make it an exciting place to live and work. See "Promotions and Duty Assignment" and "Details and Accomplishments of Duty Assignments" headings for detailed employment information.

Police Executive Research Forum
1992 to Present
Participate as a consultant for on-site management studies of police departments across the United States; research and write detailed reports regarding various aspects of these agencies' operations and administrative practices and recommend improvements as necessary.

Prince George's Community College
1997 to Present
Serve as an adjunct faculty member in the college's criminal justice program.

Thomas V. Miller, Jr., Attorney at Law
1975 to 1976
Worked as a legal secretary, performing general office and clerical duties.

Vallario & Keiffer, Attorneys at Law
1974 to 1975
Worked as a legal secretary, performing general office and clerical duties.

PROFESSIONAL ORGANIZATIONS

- Maryland Chiefs of Police Association.
- Police Chief's Association of Prince George's County.
- Prince George's County Command Officers Association.
- Mid-Atlantic Association of Women in Law Enforcement.
- Leadership Prince George's Alumni Association.
- The Johns Hopkins University Alumni Association.
- University of Maryland University College Alumni Association.
- American Society of Law Enforcement Trainers, 1990–1993.

SELECTED HONORS AND AWARDS

Women of Achievement in Prince George's County History
1994
Featured in a book that profiles exemplary women whose accomplishments have been instrumental in shaping the county's 300-year history.

Prince George's County Police Department
1992
Chief's Award for development and implementation of the Citizens Police Academy.

Mid-Atlantic Association of Women in Law Enforcement
1990
Outstanding Service Award.

Outstanding Young Women of America
1987
Selected as an "Outstanding Young Woman in America."

National Conference of Christians and Jews
1985
Citation for contributions to improved human relations.

Prince George's County Jaycees
1983
Outstanding Young Marylander Award.

Rotary Club of Southern Prince George's County
1978
Sergeant Joseph K. Brown Award for highest scholastic average in police recruit class, Session 54.

Letters of Commendation and Appreciation
1976 to Present
One hundred fifty-seven letters of commendations and appreciation available for review upon request.

DIAL, David E.
[Home Address]
[Home Phone]
[Work Phone]

EDUCATION

1980   Master of public administration. University of Colorado, Denver. Graduated with distinction.

1967   Bachelor of arts in law enforcement and administration. San Jose State College, San Jose, California.

Other Education   Graduate of the Senior Management Institute for Police, sponsored by the Police Executive Research Forum; Federal Bureau of Investigation National Academy; Rocky Mountain Program for Senior Executives in State and Local Government, University of Colorado Graduate School of Public Affairs; Police Executive Development, Pennsylvania State University; Law Enforcement Executive Development Seminar, Federal Bureau of Investigation; and numerous other management and technical seminars.

PROFESSIONAL EXPERIENCE

May 1990 to Present   Chief of Police, Naperville, Illinois (population 123,000). Naperville is located 30 miles west of Chicago and is one of the fastest growing communities in the United States. Hired after a national employment search by the International Association of Chiefs of Police. The police department has a budget of $18.6 million and 275 employees. It is accredited by the Commission for Accreditation of Law Enforcement Agencies and delivers a high level of police service to a knowledgeable and demanding public. The department has been a leader in the provision of several innovative community-oriented services and the residents enjoy a very low crime rate.

149

March 1985 to April 1990	Assistant Chief of Police, Lakewood, Colorado (population 135,000). Lakewood is a suburban community in the Denver, Colorado metropolitan area. The Lakewood Police Department is a nationally accredited law enforcement agency and has a national reputation for innovation. Responsibilities included overall direction and coordination of the three major functional divisions in the department, and direction of crime prevention and emergency preparedness activities. Served as acting chief of police during chief's absences.
January 1983 to March 1985	Police Captain, Lakewood, Colorado. Commanded the Patrol and the Administrative Services Divisions. The Patrol Division provides police patrol and animal control services to the community. The Administrative Services Division is responsible for internal affairs, training, criminalistics, records, police evidence control and budget coordination.
December 1976 to January 1983	Police Lieutenant, Lakewood, Colorado. Commanded the following sections: Crimes Against Persons—responsible for investigation of homicides, assaults, sex assaults, and juvenile-related offenses; General Investigations—responsible for investigation of burglaries, thefts, frauds, arsons and other miscellaneous offenses; Burglary Reporting and Neutralization Detail—a specialized federally funded unit designed to target and reduce burglaries in a specific area of the city; Personnel Investigations—responsible for the investigation of police misconduct allegations; and Patrol Watch Commander—responsible for managing five teams of police officers (45 employees) who provided citywide patrol services during assigned watch hours.
January 1974 to December 1976	Police Sergeant, Lakewood, Colorado. Responsible for supervision, motivation and training of a team of eight police officers who provided patrol services to the community.

May 1973 to January 1974	Police Agent, Lakewood, Colorado. Served as a patrol officer assigned to specific areas within the city.
January 1967 to May 1973	Police Officer, Milpitas, California (population approximately 30,000 at that time). Milpitas is a suburban community in the California Bay Area. Served as patrol officer and a traffic enforcement officer. Military leave from September 1967 to September 1969.
September 1967 to September 1969	Commissioned Officer, United States Army. Served as a Military Intelligence Officer in 9th Infantry Division in Vietnam. Awarded three Bronze Stars, Army Commendation Medal, National Defense Service Medal, Vietnam Service Medal, Vietnam Campaign Medal, Vietnam Gallantry Cross and Civil Action Medal.
BACKGROUND SUMMARY	Thirty-one years of comprehensive law enforcement experience ranging from beat officer to police chief. Successful management record of improving employee productivity, morale and organizational efficiency. Communicates openly with employees, citizens and the press. Has aided in the development of a positive police service image in the community, implemented a community-oriented policing philosophy, and led police agency through accreditation process. Successful record and experience in financial management in both growth and a "cutback" environment.
PROFESSIONAL EXPERIENCE	Experience as a college instructor teaching criminal justice and management courses; responsible for assisting in development of countywide arrest standards; service as a police representative on countywide adult diversion council; service as president of a local community service organization, president of two separate police planning organizations, and chairman of regional narcotics enforcement group. Member of Police Executive

151

Research Forum, International Association of Chiefs of Police and two separate county police chiefs' organizations.

PERSONAL   Date of Birth: [DATE]
DATA   Married, two adult children.

HARRY P. DOLAN
[Home Address]
[Home Telephone]
[Work Telephone]

EDUCATION

1996 — Master's Degree, Organizational Leadership and Management, University of North Carolina at Pembroke

1991 — Certified Public Manager, National Certified Public Managers Consortium, North Carolina Office of State Personnel

1990 — Police Executive Development Program Institute of Government, University of North Carolina at Chapel Hill

1980 — Bachelor of Science Degree, Criminal Justice, Western Carolina University

PROFESSIONAL EXPERIENCE

4/19/98
to present

POLICE CHIEF
Grand Rapids, Michigan

Grand Rapids is a community of 200,000 located in Southwest Michigan. The Grand Rapids Police Department is composed of 387 sworn officers and 63 civilian employees.

Currently developing a five-year strategic plan to develop community-oriented government services throughout the city.

1992–1998

POLICE CHIEF
Lumberton, North Carolina

Lumberton is a multiracial community located in Southeastern North Carolina. Lumberton is the county seat and serves as the hub for the region's commercial and industrial activity. The county population is evenly distributed among Native American, African American and Caucasian communities. The police department is composed of 67 sworn officers and 10 civilian employees, serving a population of 20,000.

Implemented the community-oriented policing philosophy throughout the city. Responsible for the development of the following initiatives: problem solving, foot and bicycle patrols, decentralized community police stations, community surveys, community meetings, school resource officer program, community policing television show, citizen police academy, increased female and minority representation, emergency special response team, major crimes and narcotics investigative team, and other innovative programs.

1987–1992   POLICE CHIEF
North Carolina Department of Human Resources (DHR) Police Department
Black Mountain, North Carolina

The DHR Police Department is a progressive law enforcement agency that provides police services in a campus setting to three state facilities: Juvenile Evaluation Center, Alcohol and Drug Treatment Center, and a mental health facility. The state complex is located within the Black Mountain and Swannanoa communities in Western North Carolina.

Responsible for reorganizing the department, establishing a progressive training program, and developing comprehensive policies and procedures. Served as a business manager at one of the state facilities for one year, and led the support services division to regain hospital accreditation status.

1982–1987   **FIRST CLASS POLICE OFFICER**
Raleigh, North Carolina, Police Department

Assigned to the Field Operations Division. Served as an instructor in the police academy and was responsible for training and supervising police recruits during the field training process. Conducted research into operational areas as requested by platoon commanders. Involved in virtually every aspect of community police service.

1980–1982   **DEPUTY SHERIFF**
Buncombe County Sheriff's Department
Asheville, North Carolina

Served as a deputy sheriff assigned to a specialized Traffic Safety Unit. Involved in a wide variety of traffic, law enforcement and major accident investigations.

PERSONAL DATA

Born [DATE]
Married, three children

EDWARD A. FLYNN

Chief of Police, Arlington County, Virginia (pop. 187,000). Appointed November 10, 1997. Arlington County is a full-service urban county of 26 square miles, located across the Potomac River from Washington, D.C. Its daytime population is more than 260,000. The police department is nationally accredited, has an authorized strength of 362 sworn and 170 non-sworn personnel, with a $36 million annual budget. The department has been reorganized to facilitate the adoption of a community-oriented policing strategy emphasizing geographic accountability and the use of problem-solving tactics.

EDUCATION

Ph.D. Program in Criminal Justice (Credits completed 1988)
Graduate Center City University of New York.

Master of Arts in Criminal Justice (1976)
John Jay College of Criminal Justice, New York, New York.

Bachelor of Arts in History (1970)
La Salle University, Philadelphia, Pennsylvania.

Leadership Washington (Class of 1998–99)
A leadership development program presented in a series of interactive forums for a group of 60 regional leaders drawn from the public, private, and not-for-profit sectors, and committed to improving the quality of life in the Metropolitan Washington region.

Program for Senior Executives in State and Local Government (1996)
Harvard University, John F. Kennedy School of Government, Cambridge, Massachusetts. An intensive three-week program based on the case-study method. Awarded a National Institute of Justice Pickett Fellowship.

Federal Bureau of Investigation National Academy (1989—157th session) Eleven-week senior command and staff school for police executives conducted at the FBI Academy, Quantico, VA.

LAW ENFORCEMENT EXPERIENCE

Chief of Police, Chelsea, MA (pop. est. 36,000). Appointed June 1993. Chelsea is a distressed city whose municipal charter had been suspended by the Commonwealth of Massachusetts when the city became bankrupt. Its population is contained in two square miles and was afflicted with a high crime rate. It is surrounded by Boston. The police department had an authorized strength of 80 sworn officers and 15 civilians. The operating budget was $4.1 million. Appointed by the receiver of Chelsea for the express purpose of professionalizing the department, restoring its credibility (in the wake of federal trials of some local politicians and police officers), developing policies and procedures, and improving the department's relations with minority communities. Implemented a problem-oriented strategy emphasizing decentralization, territoriality, job enrichment and accountability. Aggressively pursued federal and state grants, receiving more than $2 million. Successfully instituted crime reduction and fear reduction tactics. Organized neighborhoods to strengthen their capacity to resist crime and overcome disorder. The Chelsea Police Department was acknowledged as a regional leader in the community policing movement and the City of Chelsea was named an "All American City" in 1998.

Chief of Police, Braintree, MA (pop. 35,000). Appointed January 1988. The Braintree Police Department had an authorized strength of 80 sworn officers and 8 civilian employees. The operating budget was approximately $4.1 million. Braintree's 14 square miles contained more than

100,000 people each day due to its proximity to Boston and its several regional shopping centers, office complexes and hotels. Hired after a national employment search conducted by the International Association of Chiefs of Police Executive Search Service, for the specific purpose of implementing extensive operational, organizational, and administrative changes. Reorganized the department, upgraded its equipment inventory, introduced joint-venture in-house training programs, and computerized operations. Significantly improved community, interagency, intergovernmental and press relations. The Braintree Police Department was recognized as one of the most progressive suburban police agencies in the state.

Jersey City Police Department (1973–1988). Jersey City, NJ, is a racially and ethnically diverse city of 14 square miles with a population of 230,000. Located directly across the Hudson River from New York City's lower Manhattan, and connected to it by the Holland Tunnel, Jersey City is a densely populated heterogeneous environment, characterized by pockets of extreme poverty coupled with a serious crime problem. During my tenure the UCR Crime Index was approximately 17,000 crimes per year. The police department employed more than 900 officers. Promotions were the result of a competitive testing process administered by the New Jersey Department of Civil Service.

Inspector. Promoted January 1988. Responsible for conducting formal staff inspections to ensure management control over the total department's operations and personnel, and to make certain that line supervisors were effectively discharging their responsibilities.

Captain. Promoted June 1985. Commander of the Emergency Communications Division. This division received and dispatched more than 330,000 calls for service each year. Before assuming this command, was in charge of the Police Fiscal Unit, assisting with developing and managing the $38 million police budget.

Lieutenant. Promoted July 1981. Commanded the Homicide Squad and then the Street Crimes Unit. The 10-member Homicide Squad investigated an average of 40 homicides a year. The Street Crime Unit consisted of three narcotics squads and three robbery squads, and was assigned six sergeants and 30 detectives.

Sergeant. Promoted April 1977. Served in the Bureau of Patrol as a supervisor of the uniformed patrol officers assigned to the districts.

Police Officer. Appointed February 1973. Assigned to the Patrol Bureau. Served in uniformed foot patrol, marked radio car patrol, and plain clothes anti-crime patrol in the highest crime district in the city.

Police Officer. Hillside Township, NJ, Police Department. Appointed May 1971. Hillside is a densely populated community of 25,000 people in two square miles, bordering Newark, New Jersey. Assigned to general patrol duties in the 70-officer police department.

OTHER PROFESSIONAL AFFILIATIONS

Police Executive Research Forum. Treasurer and member of the Board of Directors. The Police Executive Research Forum (PERF) is a national membership organization of progressive police executives from the largest city, county and state law enforcement agencies. PERF is dedicated to improving policing and advancing professionalism through research and involvement in public policy debate.

* Gary P. Hayes Memorial Award Recipient, presented at 1999 Annual PERF Conference. Selected by the trustees of the Hayes Memorial Fund, the award is given annually "to someone who recognizes the broad nature of the police function, and engages the community and police professionals in bringing about change...the award honors a police practitioner of vision and commitment who is imaginative, open, willing to speak out on important matters, and able to enlist others in carrying out his or her commitment." The award has been conferred annually since 1986.

International Association of Chiefs of Police. Member of the Education and Training Committee, which plans the workshops offered at the annual conferences of this 15,000-member professional organization. Faculty member in IACP's training program, lecturing on community policing, leadership and ethics. Conduct organizational improvement studies for IACP Management Services Division.

Campaign for an Effective Crime Policy, Steering Committee Member. Located in Washington, D.C., the Campaign is a nonpartisan national coalition of criminal justice professionals, academics, elected officials and other public leaders who support and encourage policy making based on sound research and evaluation of anticrime strategies, and on the experience of frontline practitioners and community leaders.

Fight Crime—Invest in Kids, National Advisory Committee. Fight Crime—Invest in Kids is a nonpartisan organization that helps the public understand the scientific evidence that, in the long run, investments in children and youth are critical to our efforts to cut crime, and advocates for policies that reflect this idea.

National Community Oriented Policing Resource Board Member. Appointed by the director of the Office of the Community Oriented Police Services of the Department of Justice. NCOPRB is made up of representatives from policing agencies, community groups, respected academics and researchers to advise the director regarding funding and research priorities of the COPS Office.

Instructor of Criminal Justice, William Paterson College and Jersey City State College (September 1978 to June 1987)

ROBERT CRUMP WHITE
[Home Address, Work Phone, Home Phone]

GREENSBORO POLICE DEPARTMENT • GREENSBORO, N.C.
JUNE 1, 1998–PRESENT

POLICE CHIEF
Greensboro encompasses more than 107 square miles and has a resident population of more than 205,000. The Greensboro Police Department provides full-service community policing to the city and its residents. The department is composed of 478 sworn and 138 civilian members. The annual department budget is $35.7 million. The department provides the full range of police services to the community in concert and cooperation with the entire city government. It is dedicated to the provision of this service utilizing the community policing concept.

METROPOLITAN POLICE DEPARTMENT • WASHINGTON, D.C.
DECEMBER 1997–MAY 1998

ASSISTANT POLICE CHIEF (PATROL OPERATIONS OFFICER)
The Metropolitan Police Department is the primary law enforcement agency for the District of Columbia, a city of more than 550,000 residents. The department has more than 3,600 sworn members. The city is geographically divided into seven police districts. Its budget is more than $250 million per year. Responsible for the direct supervision of the city's seven police districts, comprising more than 2,600 sworn members, 72 percent of the department's total complement of sworn personnel. Responsible for carrying out and enhancing the department's new patrol service area model, which in 1997 contributed to a 19 percent decrease in reported crime, the largest reduction among major city police departments. Implemented a "Door to Door Campaign," requiring patrol officers to acquaint or reacquaint themselves with every resident or business owner in their patrol area. Established a "Community Government" approach to the abatement of open-air drug markets. This plan utilizes the resources of multiple government agencies in a collaborative approach to the eradication of the problem and its causes.

DISTRICT OF COLUMBIA HOUSING AUTHORITY • WASHINGTON, D.C.
SEPTEMBER 1995–DECEMBER 1997

POLICE CHIEF
Responsible for the establishment of the Office of Public Safety for the District of Columbia Housing Authority. The authority manages public housing for 55 developments, more than 11,000 dwelling units serving more than 25,000 residents. Within 90 days of appointment to this position, developed a "Comprehensive Plan To Increase Security For The Residents of Public Housing." This plan included a multifaceted approach to providing security in public housing. It is a community-based policing approach joining the existing services provided by the Metropolitan Police Department with a full range of law enforcement services provided by the housing authority. The housing authority will create a 150-person police department and a housing authority security force numbering 70. The plan includes: residential police officers living and working in housing developments; nonresidential police officers permanently assigned to housing developments; hiring police cadets (residents of public housing) as assistants to residential officers; employing resident building monitors to control entrances and exits; developing an internal security force to provide enhanced patrols to public housing; entering into collaborative partnerships with local and federal law enforcement agencies to attack narcotics-infested developments; conducting a complete physical security analysis of all developments, and establishing two mini-police stations in public housing. Managed an annual budget of more than $8 million.

METROPOLITAN POLICE DEPARTMENT • WASHINGTON, D.C.
1972–1995

COMMANDER (May 1993–September 1995)
Commanding Officer, Fourth District: Managed police service delivery for the most populous (108,000) and culturally diverse area of Washington, D.C. Oversaw a staff of 438 sworn officers and 55 civilians. Enhanced community empowerment policing and formulated department wide standards by: decentralizing operational units; designing and initiating permanent work shifts for patrol officers; establishing neighborhood beat profiles; publishing a community newsletter; implementing an awareness program for the Latino population about alcohol and vending violations; creating an after school learning center and a police-community substation; establishing a bicycle patrol; creating a summer arts and en-

richment camp for children; designing and initiating a dedicated two-way communication system for "Citizens on Patrol" groups; establishing a computerized citizen complaint tracking system; and designing and distributing crime prevention pamphlets, in five languages, to all businesses. Initiated computerized databases for business and detective case files. Created trimonthly anti-crime initiatives. Results of these actions are a policing district with a quality of police service and resident satisfaction levels far higher than other sections of the city.

INSPECTOR (MAJOR) (March 1992–May 1993)
Director, Planning and Research Division: Supervised the opening of two new police substations; redesigned and directed the operation of the Command Information Center for the 1993 Presidential Inaugural and major community disturbances; reorganized the Planning and Research Division to include establishing a new evaluation unit; continued the implementation of accreditation and community empowerment policing; served as liaison to the chief on various boards and initiatives. Managed annual budget of more than $3 million.

CAPTAIN (May 1985–March 1992)
Branch Commander, Special Operations Division, Emergency Response Team (June 1987–March 1992): Responsible for the successful resolution of more than 600 barricades, hostage situations and service of high-risk warrants without incident; annually directed a nationwide SWAT competition; directed both field training and command post exercise regionally; directed the design and secured the acquisition of a new command bus, barricade truck, bomb truck and hostage negotiator van; established a new selection criteria for members of the Emergency Response Team; established a new mandatory physical fitness program for team members.

Commander, Narcotics Branch (July 1986–June 1987): Coordinated citywide narcotic investigations and interdiction; responsible for all major narcotic investigations conducted in the city; established new procedures for the handling of narcotic cases.

Section Commander, Sixth District (May 1985–July 1986): Served as a supervisor of Uniformed Patrol in two of the three neighborhood sections (or areas) of the district; served as the support commander, which included acting as the district commander in the commander's absence.

OFFICER–LIEUTENANT (1972–1985)

Served successfully as a patrol officer (1972–1977); uniformed sergeant, Fifth District (1977–1978); robbery squad sergeant (1978–1979); uniform lieutenant, Second District (1979–1981); lieutenant, Special Operations Division, Special Events Branch (1981–1983); lieutenant, Office of the Chief of Police; short-term confidential assignment, investigation of public corruption (1983); lieutenant, Special Operations Division, Special Tactics Branch (1984); lieutenant, Community Services Coordinator, Third District (1984–1985).

EXPERIENCE/PROFESSIONAL ACCOMPLISHMENTS

Recipient of the Silver Medal of Valor (1990). Received more than 100 individual commendations. Lecturer at the University of the District of Columbia (1994), Illinois Tactical Association (1989), and Rochester Police Department (1990). Performed as an assessor in the promotional process for Baltimore City and Maryland State Police Departments, and participated as a role player for the Metropolitan Police Department.

PROFESSIONAL ORGANIZATIONS

Member of Police Executive Research Forum; International Association of Chiefs of Police; Metropolitan Police Officials Association; Organization of Black Metropolitan Police Officials; Tactical Response Association, Washington, D.C. Chapter; Illinois Tactical Response Association, Chicago, Illinois; Boy Scouts of America.

BOARDS AND COMMISSIONS

Council of Governments (1992–1993); Committee to Promote D.C. (1992–1993).

EDUCATION

Master of Science, Applied Behavioral Science, Johns Hopkins University, May 1996.

Bachelor of Arts, Public Administration, University of the District of Columbia, Summa Cum Laude 1993.

ADDITIONAL EDUCATION

George Washington University's Contemporary Executive Development Program (1991); United States Secret Service Dignitary Protection Briefing, Washington, D.C. (1981).

PERSONAL DATA

Date of Birth: [DATE]
Married: [SPOUSE NAME]
Three Children: [CHILDREN'S NAMES AND AGES]

Sample Employment Agreements and Performance Contracts

Employee Performance Contract—Example 1

WHEREAS, the City Council of the City of [CITY], a municipal corporation, has authorized an Employment Performance Contract with Police Chief [NAME], the conditions of which are set forth under the authority of Ordinance [NUMBER]; and

WHEREAS, City Manager finds it beneficial to execute this Employment Performance Contract with [NAME]; and [NAME], recognizing the benefits of this contract, agrees to enter into this contract.

NOW, THEREFORE, in consideration of the agreements contained herein, the City Manager, acting on behalf of the City of [CITY] agrees as follows:

1.   [NAME] shall work to attain the following performance goals during the next annual year.

(1)

(2)

(3)

2.   [NAME] shall receive a 180-day notice of termination by the City Manager or designee, providing he/she is willing and able to perform the duties of his/her position. The city shall compensate $[AMOUNT] in an amount equal to 180 working days salary. In the event the City Manager determines that [NAME] should not continue to perform his/her duties, even though he/she may be willing and able to perform his/her duties, [NAME] will receive payment in the amount of 180 working days' salary.

3.   In the event the employee is charged with a felony, he/she shall not be entitled to any compensation as provided in paragraph 2 above if terminated.

4. In the event [NAME] voluntarily resigns his/her position with the City, he/she shall not be entitled to any compensation as provided in paragraph 2 above.

IN WITNESS WHEREOF, the City of [CITY] has caused this agreement to be executed by its City Manager and duly attested by its City Clerk, and [NAME] has executed this agreement. Dated this [DATE] day of [MONTH], [YEAR].

CITY OF [CITY], a municipal corporation

By: _____
    City Manager

ATTEST:

_____
City Clerk

_____
Date

Police Chief Employment Agreement—Example 2

This AGREEMENT is made and entered into by and between the CITY OF [CITY], [STATE], a municipal corporation duly organized under the laws of the State of [STATE], hereinafter referred to as "CITY" and [NAME], hereinafter referred as "Employee".

WITNESSETH

WHEREAS, City desires to employ the services of Employee as Police Chief for the City of [CITY]; and

WHEREAS, both City and Employee agree that it is appropriate to enter into this Agreement in order to provide benefits, conditions of employment and the term of employment; and

WHEREAS, Employee desires to accept employment as Police Chief for the City of [CITY], and

WHEREAS, Employee and City acknowledge that this Agreement is made in the context of the "Rules and Regulations of the City of [CITY]" and the "Memorandum of Personnel Understanding between the City of [CITY] and the Management/Confidential Employees" (hereinafter "MOU"), and that the provisions thereof shall supersede any conflicting provision of this Agreement.

NOW, THEREFORE, the City of [CITY] does hereby employ the services of [NAME] as its Chief of Police under and in accord with the following terms and conditions:

SECTION 1. DUTIES AND RESPONSIBILITIES

A. As Chief of Police, the Employee shall be the Chief Executive Officer of the Police Department. The Employee shall be responsible for planning, organizing, directing, staffing and coordinating police operations. The Employee shall be responsible for reporting the operational performance of the Police Department, budget preparation, labor negotiations, personnel administration and disaster preparedness.

B. The Employee shall perform such other duties and functions as the City Manager shall from time to time assign.

C. The Employee shall formulate departmental rules, regulations and procedures in cooperation with the City Manager, to whom the Employee reports and to whom the Employee is responsible for the proper operation of the Police Department.

D. The Employee shall devote his/her entire time to the discharge of official duties and shall not engage in outside employment without the prior written approval of the City Manager pursuant to the Rules.

E. The Employee shall become certified as a law enforcement officer in [STATE] as expeditiously as possible and shall comply with all statutory requirements for holding the office of Chief of Police. The City shall provide necessary time to attend certification exams and classes if any are required by the State of [STATE].

SECTION 2. TERM OF EMPLOYMENT

The term of this Agreement shall be for thirty-six (36) months, commencing on [DATE] and terminating on [DATE (three years later)], subject to the Rules and the MOU including the required one-year probationary period. Nevertheless, the parties may extend the term of Employee's employment beyond [DATE], by a written amendment to this Agreement. For that purpose, the parties shall undertake discussion on or about [DATE (one year before expiration date)], provided that neither party shall be required to agree to extend the term of Employee's employment.

SECTION 3. SALARY AND BENEFITS

A. Salary. City shall pay Employee for his/her services on an annual base salary of $[AMOUNT], payable in bi-weekly installments made at the same time as other city employees. City agrees to increase this salary in the same increments as any other general wage increase provided to other Management employees.

B. Salary Adjustments and Benefits. The Employee is entitled to the salary adjustments and benefits provided for in the MOU. In addition, City agrees to increase the salary and/or other benefits of Employee in such amounts and to such extent as the City Manager may determine on the basis of an annual salary or benefit review consistent with the salary ranges permitted by the MOU. In addition, the Employee shall be reimbursed for any reasonable costs for relocation not to exceed $2,500.00.

SECTION 4. PERFORMANCE EVALUATION

A. The City Manager shall review and evaluate the performance of the Employee at least once annually. The Employee shall be entitled to discuss the evaluation fully with the Manager.

B. The City Manager shall hold the evaluation of the Employee's job performance on or about the employment anniversary each year.

C. The City Manager will consider in the performance evaluation all relevant factors, including but not limited to the City's Rules and MOU and the following:

- Progress toward achieving departmental goals and objectives;

- Leadership effectiveness;

- Managerial skills to include utilization of the department's financial and human resources;

- Oral and written communication skills;

- Working relationships with the community, City department heads, employee organizations and the news media;

- Openness of police operations and responsiveness in addressing crime and service problems of concern to the community;

- Integrity;

- Creativity and innovation;

- Professional development and involvement.

SECTION 5. AUTOMOBILE

A. The Council shall provide Employee with the exclusive use of an automobile.

B. The Council shall pay for liability, property damage and comprehensive insurance, and for the purchase, maintenance, repair and regular replacement of said automobile for business-related purposes.

C. The Council shall procure and maintain an automobile liability insurance policy on the automobile in, at least, the minimum coverage required by law.

SECTION 6. PROFESSIONAL DEVELOPMENT

A. Dues and Subscriptions. City agrees to pay an appropriate amount for the professional dues and subscriptions of employee.

B. Training, Education and Professional Involvement. City hereby agrees to pay an appropriate amount to be determined by the City Manager for travel and subsistence expenses of Employee for professional and official travel, meetings and occasions. The amount shall be adequate to continue the professional development of Employee and to adequately pursue necessary official and other functions for City.

SECTION 7. INDEMNIFICATION

City acknowledges that Employee is an employee of the City of [CITY] and that Employee is entitled to all of the immunities and protections available under the Governmental Tort Claim Act. In addition, City and Employee shall be subject to the provisions of Article 4 of Chapter 1 of Part 2 of Division 3.6 of the [STATE] Government Code and Part 7 of Division 3.6 of the [STATE] Government Code.

SECTION 8. TERMINATION

The City may terminate the Employee before the expiration of the aforesaid term of employment pursuant to Rules and the MOU. In addition, the City may terminate the Employee without cause but, in that event, Employee shall be entitled to receive severance pay equal to four (4) months as his/her sole and exclusive compensation for the termination of his/her employment with City. The employee may terminate his employment by giving thirty (30) days written notice to the City Manager.

If Employee dies during the term of his/her employment, City shall pay to Employee's estate all compensation that would otherwise be payable to the Employee up to the date of the Employee's death and the contract shall terminate as of such date.

SECTION 9. EFFECT OF RULES AND REGULATIONS AND MEMORANDUM OF UNDERSTANDING

City and Employee acknowledge that this Agreement is subject to all of the provisions of "Personnel Rules and Regulations of the City of [CITY]" and the "Memorandum of Understanding between the City of [CITY] and Management/Confidential Employees" and that the provisions of said documents shall supersede and control any conflicting provision of this Agreement.

SECTION 10. OTHER TERMS AND CONDITIONS OF EMPLOYMENT

A.   Agreement Modification. The City in consultation with Employee, may modify, amend or fix such other terms and conditions of employment as may be determined, from time to time, to be necessary or appropriate, provided that such terms and conditions are not inconsistent or in conflict with the provisions of this agreement or any other applicable law.

B.   Complete Agreement. The provisions of this Agreement constitute the entire agreement between the parties. No representation or understanding, whether communicated orally or on writing, is or shall be effective unless contained in this Agreement.

C.   Agreement Binding. This Agreement shall be binding upon and inure to the benefit of the heirs at law and executors of Employee.

D.   If any provision, or portion thereof, contained in this Agreement is held unconstitutional, invalid or unenforceable, the remainder of this Agreement, or portion thereof, shall be deemed severable, shall not be affected and shall remain in full force and effect.

IN WITNESS OF THE FOREGOING, the parties have set their hands on [DATE] in [CITY], [STATE].

CITY: EMPLOYEE:

_____   _____
[NAME], Mayor   [NAME]

ATTEST:

_____
[NAME], City Clerk

APPROVED AS TO FORM:

_____
[NAME], City Attorney

Employment Agreement—Example 3

THIS AGREEMENT, effective [DATE] by and between the City of [CITY], a chartered municipal corporation, hereinafter "City" and [NAME], hereinafter "Employee".

RECITALS

1. City desires to employ the services of [NAME] as Police Chief of the city of [CITY] to perform the duties set forth in Article [XX], of the Charter of the city of [CITY];

2. It is the desire of the Mayor and City Council to provide the benefits and establish the conditions of employment for [NAME];

3. It is the desire of the Mayor and City Council to provide inducement for [NAME] to accept and remain in such employment and to encourage full work productivity and administrative stability and independence by assuring [NAME]'s morale and peace of mind with respect to future security;

4. [NAME] desires to accept employment as Police Chief of said City.

NOW, THEREFORE, in consideration of the mutual promises set forth herein, the parties agree as follows:

SECTION 1. DUTIES

1.1 City agrees to employ [NAME] as Police Chief to perform the functions and duties set forth in Article [XX], Section [XX] of the City Charter of the City of [CITY].

SECTION 2. TERM

2.1 The term of employment shall commence on [DATE], and shall continue until [DATE (three years later)], unless sooner terminated by the parties pursuant to this agreement.

2.2 City may terminate Employee at any time.

2.3 Employee may resign from employment at any time upon giving four (4) months written notice to City during the original term of this agreement, or one (1) month's written notice during any renewal term; provided, however, that notice shall not be required in the event Employee resigns pursuant to a request for resignation by City, or after receiving notice of City's intent not to renew this agreement pursuant to Section 3.1.

SECTION 3. RENEWAL TERMS

3.1 This agreement shall be renewed automatically for successive periods of one year (renewal term), unless the City gives Employee written notice not less than 30 days prior to the expiration of the original term as set forth in Section 2.1 or any renewal term, of City's intent not to renew this agreement.

SECTION 4. ACTS ENTITLING EMPLOYEE TO SEVERANCE COMPENSATION

4.1 Employee shall be entitled to severance compensation set forth in Section 5 in the following events:
(a) The City elects not to renew this agreement pursuant to Section 3.1.
(b) The City terminates Employee without cause as defined in Section 10.
(c) The City requests the resignation of Employee, and Employee resigns pursuant to such request.

SECTION 5. SEVERANCE COMPENSATION

5.1 In the event Employee's employment ceases pursuant to Section 4, City shall pay the salary and benefits set forth in Sections 6 and 7 of this Agreement for a period of twelve (12) months, or until Employee obtains other employment, whichever occurs first.

SECTION 6. SALARY

6.1 Commencing [DATE], City agrees to pay an annual salary of [Amount], payable in installments and at the same time that other City employees are paid.

SECTION 7. BENEFITS

7.1 Automobile. City shall provide Employee with a telephone-equipped Mazda 929, or its equivalent, for both business use and the personal use of Employee and those dependents residing with him/her who hold valid [STATE] drivers licenses. City shall pay all liability, property damage and comprehensive insurance coverage, and for the purchase, operation (including all fuels and lubricants), maintenance, repair and replacement every two years from the anniversary day of this agreement.

7.2 Expenses and dues. City shall pay all reasonable and necessary business expenses, including dues in civic organizations. Employee shall submit such expenses pursuant to Section [XX] of the Charter of the City of [CITY].

7.3 Retirement contribution. City shall pay an amount equal to 20 percent of Employee's salary to the ICMA Retirement Fund.

7.4 Travel expenses. City shall pay all travel, accommodation and food expenses incurred by Employee for conferences and seminars associated or related to city business or professional training and development. Such reimbursement shall be subject to Resolution No. [XX] or any amendment thereto.

7.5 Professional leave. Employee shall be entitled to ten (10) days leave each year for the purposes of teaching, consulting or speaking. Such leave shall not accumulate, and to the extent such leave is not used in any year it shall lapse.

7.6 Vacation and sick leave. Employee shall be credited with thirty (30) days of sick leave and eighteen (18) days vacation on [DATE (of employment)], and will earn vacation leave at the rate of eighteen (18) days each calendar year, until Employee has earned a maximum vacation leave of 54 days each calendar year. To the extent Employee utilizes vacation leave in any calendar year, he/she shall be entitled to recapture such used vacation leave at the rate of 1.5 days per month, but in no event shall such recapture exceed 54 vacation leave days in any calendar year. Example: Employee is entitled to 54 calendar days vacation leave. Employee uses 10 days vacation leave in January, thereby reducing his/her remaining leave to 44 days. Beginning in February, he/she will earn 1.5 days of vacation leave per month, until he/she has reached a maximum vacation leave of

54 days in that calendar year. Employee may receive compensation for all unused vacation leave credit and sick leave credit up to a maximum of two years.

7.7 Long term disability policy. Employee presently has and maintains a long term disability income policy with [Name of Company], policy no. [XX]. City shall pay the premiums on said policy as they become due, or pay to Employee an amount equal to the premiums at the time they become due.

7.8 Reimbursement of Social Security payments. City shall reimburse Employee an amount equal to the periodic deductions made for Social Security purposes.

7.9 Management benefits not otherwise provided. Except as otherwise provided herein, all provisions of the [CITY] Municipal Code and other resolutions, policies, rules and regulations of the City relating to sick leave, retirement and pension system contributions, holidays and other fringe benefits as they now exist or may hereafter be amended, shall apply to Employee as they do to other management employees of the City.

7.10 Housing allowance. Provided Employee shall reside within the City boundaries, City shall pay to Employee the sum of $1,200 per month to pay for or offset the cost of housing that Employee will incur as a result of accepting employment with the City ("the allowance"). In the event that a residential purchase is made pursuant to the provisions of paragraph 7.10 of this agreement, the allowance will be reduced in proportion to the federal and state tax benefits received as a result of such purchase. Example: A residential purchase is made for a total consideration of $400,000, and the annual interest payments are $12,000 and annual taxes are $3,000. Assuming that Employee is in the 31 percent federal tax bracket and 9 percent state tax bracket, and both the interest and taxes are deductible items on both federal and state tax returns, then the allowance shall be reduced by $500 per month ($15,000 [total deductions] X 40% [combined federal and state tax bracket]= $6,000/12 months=$500/month).

7.11 Residential purchase. At such time as Employee determines to purchase a residential dwelling in the City of [CITY] for the use of him-/herself and his/her family, the City shall pay 66-2/3 percent of the down payment, and Employee shall pay 33-1/3 percent of the down payment, but the City share shall not exceed $200,000. Title shall be taken in

Employee's name. Employee shall pay in a timely manner all mortgage payments, taxes, insurance and assessments, and shall pay all costs of maintenance, repair and replacement. Upon termination of employment with the City, or upon the residence no longer being used as the primary residence for Employee, the property shall be placed for sale no earlier than 90 days after the termination and the net proceeds divided 66-2/3 percent to the city and 33-1/3 percent to Employee. Either party may buy the interest of the other at a mutually agreeable price. It is agreed that at the time of such residential purchase the parties will execute a recordable Equity Sharing Agreement that shall provide for the terms and conditions for the reimbursement to City of its share of the down payment from the sale of the residence.

SECTION 8. TERMINATION FOR CAUSE

8.1 Notwithstanding any provision of this agreement to the contrary, City may terminate Employee without payment of severance compensation only under the following circumstances:
(a) Employee violates Sections 2.3, 9, and 11 of this Agreement.
(b) Employee is convicted of a felony or misdemeanor involving moral turpitude, which involve theft, material false statement under oath, sexual misconduct, crimes against person, e.g. battery or assault, or offenses relating to alcohol.
(c) Employee is determined by the Fair Political Practices Commission to have unlawfully participated in a governmental decision in which he/she had a conflict of interest as defined in Government Code section [XX], et seq. or by the District Attorney to have violated Government Code section [XX].

SECTION 9. RESIDENCY

9.1 Employee agrees to maintain residency within 15 miles of the boundaries of the City.

SECTION 10. PERFORMANCE EVALUATION

10.1 The City shall review and evaluate the performance of Employee six (6) months after the execution of this Agreement, and at least once annually thereafter. Said review and evaluation shall be conducted in accordance with procedures and forms and with respect to specific criteria to be developed jointly by Employee and City. Said review and evaluation shall be private and confidential, and the results shall be summarized and discussed in closed session, to the extent permitted by law, or through some other mutually acceptable closed format. The parties agree that the primary purposes of such evaluation are to facilitate open and frank discussion, define roles and expectations, identify performance strengths and weaknesses, and provide an opportunity for Employee to take affirmative action to address weaknesses and areas needing improvement.

SECTION 11. EXCLUSIVE EMPLOYMENT

11.1 Employee shall devote his/her full time, energy and efforts to the City, and shall accept no outside employment, but the foregoing shall not limit Employee in teaching, writing, lecturing, or consulting, but only to the extent that such activities do not interfere with his/her duties as set forth in Section 1.1.

SECTION 12. ENTIRE AGREEMENT

12.1 The foregoing contains the entire agreement of the parties, and no modification shall be binding upon the parties unless the same is in writing, signed by the respective parties hereto.

SECTION 13. EFFECT OF PARTIAL INVALIDITY

13.1 If any provision of this agreement is for any reason deemed illegal or unenforceable by a court of competent jurisdiction, the remaining portion shall be deemed severable and shall remain in full force and effect.

IN WITNESS WHEREOF, the City has caused this agreement to be duly executed by its Mayor and City Clerk and [NAME] has signed this agreement the [DATE] day of [MONTH], [YEAR].

CITY OF [CITY],
a chartered municipal corporation,

_____
Mayor

_____
City Clerk

APPROVED AS TO FORM:(SEAL)

_____

City Attorney

_____

[NAME]

Letter of Agreement—Example 4

[DATE]

[NAME]
[ADDRESS]

Dear [NAME]:

This is a confirmation of our conversation earlier this week. We are extremely pleased to formally offer you the position of police chief for the City of [CITY].

The key purpose of this letter is to outline the conditions of this offer.

- A starting salary of [Amount/year]. Eligibility for future increases will be based on our normal pay administration rules with your first eligibility being [DATE].

- All standard city benefits based on normal rules and program design.

- A higher than standard annual leave earnings rate of 129 hours/year (16.1 days).

- A monthly car allowance of $325 (this figure may increase in the future as it is indexed to changes in the allowable mileage reimbursement established by IRS). This allowance is to cover reasonable, local area travel for business use and you will have full personal use of your vehicle. Longer trips are reimbursed on a per-mile basis over and above the allowance.

- Reasonable relocation expenses for you and your family (we will discuss the best approach to this when the time arrives). While it is not an official city policy that department heads reside in the city limits, it is expected that you as police chief will do so within 12 months of appointment.

- A severance pay arrangement that provides you with full salary for three months should you be terminated prior to two years of employment for any reason other than illegal activity or act of moral turpitude that substantially impairs your ability to reasonably perform your duties. After two years of employment as Chief, the severance portion of this offer will be eliminated.

- Your initial day of employment will be [DATE].

- This offer is contingent on successful completion of a standard pre-employment physical exam and drug test required of all new full time employees.

- This offer is also contingent upon you becoming certified as a police officer in the state of [STATE] within one year of employment. [NAME] has talked to you briefly about this issue and we can pursue the steps necessary to achieve certification once the appointment is announced. At a minimum, you will need to complete some specific course work related to [STATE] law and be qualified with your firearm. We are starting a new Police Academy class on [DATE] and all of the potentially required courses will be taught at some point during the academy.

We have scheduled the news conference to announce your appointment for [TIME AND DATE] in the [NAME] Municipal Office Building.

I am very excited that you will be joining our organization in this crucial role. As a municipal government, we enjoy a long history of solid service delivery to the public, and the police department is specifically well thought of and supported in our community. In addition, we are rapidly developing a very strong team of top managers in the organization. We look forward to your successfully filling the role of chief in leading our department to new levels, realizing your next professional goal and also contributing as a valued member of the team as we strive to serve our citizens even better in the future. We discussed some of our expectations for the new chief during the interviews, and will be going over those in detail with you as soon as you start work.

If you need assistance with anything please contact [NAME] at [TELEPHONE NUMBER]. Otherwise we all look forward to seeing you again on [DATE].

Sincerely,

[NAME]
City Manager

Agreement and Acceptance of Employment:

[NAME]
Police Chief

Memorandum of Understanding—Example 5

This Memorandum of Understanding, made and entered into this [DATE] day of [MONTH], [YEAR] between the City of [CITY], a municipal corporation, hereinafter referred to as the Employer and [NAME], hereinafter referred to as the Employee, provides:

For and in consideration of salary and benefit payments hereinafter mentioned to be made by the City of [CITY], [NAME] agrees to act as [TITLE] for the City of [CITY]; and to carry out to the best of his/her ability duties imposed upon him/her by the general law of the State of [STATE] and the City Code of the City of [CITY] and such other duties as the City Manager of the City of [CITY] may from time to time require of him/her.

The parties agree that within ninety (90) days of execution of this Contract the Employee shall submit to the City Manager a proposed Performance Contract covering the Employee's obligations and duties under this Contract.

COMPENSATION OF EMPLOYEE

BASIC SALARY

The salary paid by the City to the Employee shall be $[AMOUNT] per year.

MEDICAL AND DENTAL INSURANCE

The City shall pay, on behalf of the Employee, the health insurance premium for the Employee and dependents not to exceed the contribution amount for the [Insurance Company] Plan B coverage.

The city shall pay, on behalf of the Employee and dependents, the dental insurance premium equal to the amount paid for other employees of the City.

The City will pay the Employee's portion for Medicare at 1.45%.

LONG-TERM DISABILITY INSURANCE

The City shall provide long-term disability insurance as provided for all executive employees of the city.

PUBLIC EMPLOYEES RETIREMENT SYSTEM (PERS)

The City will pay the full cost of the Employee's participation in the Public Employees Retirement System.

LIFE INSURANCE

The city shall pay and keep in force, during the term of this Contract, life insurance policies as provided for all executive employees of the City.

REIMBURSEMENT OF EXPENSES

The City agrees to pay on behalf of the Employee $5,000 for relocation expenses providing that should the Employee remain with the city for less than one year due to his/her voluntary resignation, he/she shall reimburse the City $5,000.

VACATION AND SICK LEAVE

The Employee shall accrue fifteen (15) days of vacation each year during the term of this agreement. Employee shall accrue twelve (12) days of sick leave each year during the term of this agreement. Employee shall be entitled to carry over unused vacation and sick leave from year to year. In the event of termination of employment, Employee shall be entitled to payment for all unused vacation leave. In the event of the termination of employment, Employee shall not be entitled to payment for unused sick leave. These leave accruals are in addition to recognized City holidays.

ADMINISTRATIVE LEAVE

The Employee shall accrue eight (8) days of administrative leave per year during the term of this agreement. Unused administrative leave can neither be reimbursed nor carried over to the next year of employment.

EXPENSES

The City agrees to budget and to pay the professional dues, license and certification fees and subscriptions of the Employee reasonably necessary for his/her continuation and full participation in national, regional, state and local associations and organizations necessary and desirable for his/her continued professional participation, growth and advancement, or for the good of the City.

The City agrees to budget and to pay the travel and subsistence expenses of the Employee for official travel, meetings and occasions reasonably adequate to continue the professional development of the Employee and to reasonably pursue necessary official and other functions for the City including, but not limited to, national, regional, state and local conferences, governmental groups and committees thereof, which Employee serves as a member.

The City shall reimburse the Employee for expenses incurred for books and tuition, upon proof of completion of class or classes satisfactorily passed, designed to increase the effectiveness of the Employee in the performance of his/her duties.

AUTOMOBILE ALLOWANCE

The Employee shall provide his/her own vehicle to be used in the performance of his/her duties and the City shall provide a car allowance of $200 per month for said use. It is anticipated that this allowance will cover all travel within the Counties of [COUNTY] and [COUNTY]. Travel outside those counties will be reimbursed to the Employee at the rate per mile paid to all other city employees except that in no case shall the mileage reimbursement for any one trip exceed the cost of coach airfare between the [NAME] Airport and the destination city and return. Employee shall furnish evidence of insurance satisfactory to the City Manager.

In certain instances when it is to the City's benefit, the City Manager may authorize the use of a City car for specific assignments.

PHYSICAL EXAMINATION

The City shall provide and pay for a physical examination for the Employee on an annual basis subject to the prior approval of the City Manager.

DUTIES OF EMPLOYEE

During the time of this agreement, the Employee shall be a full-time [TITLE] and shall not engage in outside employment nor directly or indirectly render services to any person or organization for compensation without the specific permission of the City Manager. The Employee agrees that, to the best of his ability, he/she will at all times loyally and conscientiously perform all the duties and obligations required of him/her by the terms of this Memorandum of Understanding.

GENERAL PROVISIONS

The following general provisions shall apply to this Memorandum of Understanding:

Either party may terminate this Memorandum of Understanding upon providing ninety (90) days notice.

This Memorandum of Understanding supersedes any and all other understandings, either oral or written, between the parties hereto with respect to the employment of the Employee by the City and contains all of the covenants and agreements between the parties with respect to such employment.

Each party agrees and acknowledges that no representations, inducements, promises or agreements, orally or otherwise, have been made by any party, or anyone acting on behalf of any party, that are not embodied herein and that any agreement, statement, or promises not contained in this Memorandum of Understanding shall not be valid or binding on either party.

Any modifications of this Memorandum of Understanding will be effective only if made in writing and approved by both the Employee and the City.

If any provision of this Memorandum of Understanding is held by a Court of competent jurisdiction to be invalid, void or unenforceable, the remaining provisions shall nevertheless continue in full force and effect without being impaired or invalidated in any way.

IN WITNESS WHEREOF; the parties have executed this agreement on the [DATE] day of [MONTH], [YEAR].

Police Chief Employment Agreement—Example 6

THIS AGREEMENT FOR EMPLOYMENT ("Agreement") is made and entered into this [DATE] day of [MONTH], [YEAR] between the City of [CITY] ("CITY") and [NAME], hereinafter called POLICE CHIEF, pursuant to these terms and conditions:

A.   CITY wishes to employ the services of [NAME] as the police chief of the CITY; and

B.   CITY and POLICE CHIEF desire to provide for certain procedures, benefits and requirements regarding the employment of POLICE CHIEF by the CITY; and

C.   POLICE CHIEF is willing to work as Police Chief of said CITY under the terms and conditions recited herein.

NOW, THEREFORE, CITY and POLICE CHIEF agree to the following:

SECTION 1.   Duties.

CITY agrees to retain [NAME] as POLICE CHIEF of [CITY], [STATE], to perform all duties as specified by law and ordinance, and to perform such other proper duties as assigned by the City Manager.

SECTION 2.   Compensation.

A.   The salary compensation of POLICE CHIEF shall be [AMOUNT] per annum. This is Step 6 of a seven-step salary range. Compensation thereof shall be made in equal payments biweekly consistent with employee payroll periods of CITY.

A pay increase shall be given at one-year anniversary if job performance is satisfactory or better.

B.   Benefits will be made available to POLICE CHIEF as outlined in Resolution No. [XXX], A RESOLUTION OF THE CITY OF [CITY] ESTABLISHING SALARIES AND BENEFITS FOR MANAGEMENT EMPLOYEES, and any future amendment of such resolution, a copy of which is attached to this Employment Agreement.

C.   CITY shall provide an automobile for POLICE CHIEF's exclusive use during his/her employment with CITY. CITY shall be responsible for providing liability, property damage and comprehensive insurance, and for the purchase, operation, maintenance, repair and regular replacement of POLICE CHIEF's automobile. POLICE CHIEF shall not permit his/her spouse, dependent, nor any unauthorized person to drive or use said automobile.

SECTION 3.   Term and Severance Pay.

A.   The term of this Agreement shall commence on the [DATE] day of [MONTH], [YEAR] and shall expire on the [DATE] day of [MONTH], [YEAR].

B.   If POLICE CHIEF is terminated from the employment of CITY during said term for any reason except as expressly provided herein by this Agreement, POLICE CHIEF shall be entitled to severance pay in an amount equal to six (6) months' salary based upon the annual salary of POLICE CHIEF at the time of termination (benefits other than salary as set forth in Section 2 shall not be included).

C.   POLICE CHIEF shall not be entitled to severance pay in the event that POLICE CHIEF is terminated as a result of conviction of a felony or for a crime involving moral turpitude. For purpose of resolving any dispute regarding whether the severance payment has been properly denied, CITY shall have the burden of establishing by a preponderance of evidence that POLICE CHIEF was convicted of a felony or a crime involving moral turpitude.

Notwithstanding any provision in this Agreement to the contrary, POLICE CHIEF expressly acknowledges and agrees that POLICE CHIEF is an "at will" employee and that the City Manager may exercise his/her uncontrolled discretion to remove POLICE CHIEF. POLICE CHIEF shall be given thirty (30) days' written notice of the City Manager's intent to terminate.

SECTION 4.   Notices.
Notices pursuant to this Agreement shall be given by deposit in the custody of the United States Postal Service, postage prepaid, addressed as follows:

A. CITY: City Manager
[ADDRESS]

B. POLICE CHIEF:
Police Chief
[ADDRESS]

Alternatively, notices required pursuant to this Agreement may be personally served in the same manner as is applicable to civil judicial practice. Notice shall be deemed given as of the date of personal service or as of the date of deposit of such written notice in the course of transmission in the United States Postal Service.

IN WITNESS WHEREOF, the parties hereto have caused this Agreement of Employment to be executed, in duplicate, on the day and year first above written.

CITY OF [CITY]:

_____
[NAME], Mayor

ATTEST:

_____
[NAME], City Clerk

POLICE CHIEF:

_____
[NAME]

Agreement—Example 7

THIS AGREEMENT, made and entered into on this the (date) day of (month), (year), by and between the City, a municipal corporation organized and existing under the laws of the State of (state), hereinafter called the "City" or "Employer" and (Prospective Chief), hereinafter called the Employee",

WITNESSETH:

WHEREAS, the City desires to employ the services of said Employee as Police Chief for the City; and

WHEREAS, the Employee desires to accept said employment; and

WHEREAS, it is the mutual desire of the parties to establish the term of office, benefits and conditions of employment; and

WHEREAS, it is the desire of the City:

(1) to secure and retain the services of Employee and to provide inducement for him/her to remain in such employment,

(2) to make possible full work productivity by assuring Employee's morale and peace of mind with respect to future security;

(3) to act as a deterrent against malfeasance or dishonesty for personal gain on the part of the Employee;

(4) to provide a just means for terminating Employee; and

(5) to provide a just means for terminating Employee's services at such time as he/she may be unable fully to discharge the essential functions of his/her job due to permanent disability or when City or Employee may mutually desire to otherwise terminate his/her employment.

NOW, THEREFORE, IN CONSIDERATION OF THE MUTUAL COVENANTS HEREIN CONTAINED, THE PARTIES HERETO AGREE AS FOLLOWS:

SECTION 1. DUTIES

The City hereby agrees to employ said Employee as Police Chief for the City to perform the functions and duties specified and to perform such other legally permissible and proper duties and functions incidental to employment as Police Chief.

Under the general direction of the Director of Public Safety, the Employee will represent the City as Police Chief with such duties as are set forth in the City Charter, Classified Service Rules and/or applicable ordinances, including all supplements and amendments thereto, as well as conduct his/her responsibilities pursuant to State statutes and perform other related work, as required.

SECTION 2. TERMINATION AND RESIGNATION

A.   The City may terminate this contract because of malfeasance or nonfeasance of duty, including but not limited to, undue absence affecting performance of duties, conviction of crime serious enough to affect the performance of job duties, of abusive use of alcohol or drugs, which use may impair the performance of his/her duties.

B. The Employee agrees to remain exclusively employed by the City and the City agrees to employ the Employee in accordance with the terms and conditions of this contract from [Date] until [Date] and the Employee agrees not to become employed by any other employer until the above-mentioned termination date, or any renewal thereof.

C. Nothing in this Agreement shall prevent, limit, or otherwise interfere with the right of the Employee to resign his/her position, provided the Employee gives the Employer ninety (90) days prior written notice of his/her intent to resign his/her services for the Employer.

D.   Disciplinary and/or discharge procedures shall be those set forth in the Charter and Classified Service Rules for unclassified employees.

SECTION 3. WORK WEEK

During this period, the Employee will be a full-time salaried employee. The normal work week shall include all hours required to perform the tasks assigned, and may require night and weekend hours. It is expressly understood that as a salaried employee, payments for overtime or other remuneration outside the salary set forth in Section 4 are precluded.

The term "exclusive employ" shall not be construed to include occasional teaching, writing, or consulting after normal City office hours, or during weekends, holidays and vacation days, provided such work does not impair the discharge of his/her official duties as Police Chief for the City.

SECTION 4. BEST INTERESTS

During the term of this Agreement, the Employee shall devote his/her best efforts and his/her time to advance the interests of the Employer, shall perform his/her duties to the best of his/her ability, shall work at all times for the best interests of the Employer, shall be a person of good moral character and shall uphold the office of Police Chief with dignity, integrity, honesty and dedicated responsibility to the City.

SECTION 5. SALARY

The City agrees to pay Employee for his/her services commencing on (date) an annualized base salary of ($ Amount) payable in weekly installments. Said salary is contingent upon Personnel Commission approval. The City agrees to review the amount of the base salary in accordance with the Merit Rules adopted by the Personnel Commission of the City of [Name] for unclassified employees, and any other rules or policies enacted pursuant to the Charter of the City.

SECTION 6. VACATION, SICK AND PERSONAL LEAVE BENEFITS

The City agrees to provide Employee with paid vacation and sick leave as follows:

A. Sick Leave: Ten (10) sick days per work year accruing at the rate of point eight thirty three (.833) days per month, and shall be carried over from one year to the next.

B. Vacation Leave: Ten (10) vacation days from the date of hire until [Date], thereafter twenty (20) vacation days per fiscal year commencing [Date]; these days shall be credited at the beginning of each defined period. Accrued vacation time may be carried from one fiscal year to the next with the approval of the Director of Human Resources.

C.   Personal Leave. From the date of hire until [Date] the employee will receive two (2) personal days. Each fiscal year thereafter, the employee shall be entitled to three (3) personal days. Said days may not be accumulated beyond each fiscal year.

D.   Separation of Employment: Upon non-renewal or separation of employment, said Employee will be paid out accrued vacation time only.

SECTION 7. PENSIONS

Employee acknowledges that he/she is an "unclassified employee" under the terms of this Agreement and waives any and all claims or rights to participate in the Classified Employees Retirement Fund (Pension Plan) as set forth in the City Charter. The City agrees to provide retirement payments equal to three percent (3%) of Employee's base pay, commencing upon hire and each year thereafter, into a tax sheltered annuity selected by the Employee. Said payments shall be made weekly.

SECTION 8. HEALTH AND LIFE INSURANCE

While in the employment of the City as Police Chief, the City agrees that the Employee and his/her family will receive all health insurance and life insurance equal to that provided to unclassified employees. Coverage shall commence upon hire. In addition, Employee will be responsible for employee health insurance contributions to the same extent required of unclassified employees.

SECTION 9. OTHER BENEFITS

A. The City agrees to pay the Employee up to a maximum of ten thousand ($10,000) dollars in relocation costs, such as mortgage points, moving expenses, closing costs, comparable rent or mortgage differential.

B. The City agrees to pay the Employee a yearly stipend of Nine Hundred Dollars ($900) to be used for the purchase of uniforms, cleaning of work attire or other related expenses. No invoice or other documentation will be required of the Employee to substantiate this stipend.

C. Employee's duties require that he/she shall have the use at all times during his/her employment with the Employer an automobile provided by the Employer. Said automobile shall be insured under and listed on the City's automobile liability policy. The City shall purchase, maintain, repair and regularly replace the automobile. In addition, the City agrees to pay all expenses, including gas expenses for travel and use of said automobile.

D. The Employee shall be entitled to the same holidays as those members of the [Name] supervisory union.

E. Subject to budgetary appropriation and the prior written approval of the Mayor, the Employee will be compensated and the City will pay all reasonable costs and expenses associated with work-related conferences and training, including lodging and travel expenses. Reimbursements shall be limited to the City's travel policy.

SECTION 10. OTHER TERMS AND CONDITIONS OF EMPLOYMENT

The City shall fix any other reasonable terms and conditions of employment, as it may determine from time to time, relating to the performance of Employee, provided such terms and conditions are not inconsistent with, or in conflict with, the provisions of this Agreement, the City Charter, or any other law.

SECTION 11. INDEMNIFICATION

The City shall protect and hold harmless the Employee from financial loss and expense including legal fees and costs, if any arising out of any claim, demand, suit or judgment in accordance with the provisions of Section [XXX] of the State Statutes as amended from time to time.

SECTION 12. GENERAL PROVISIONS

A. The text herein shall constitute the entire Agreement between the parties.

B. The parties acknowledge that this Agreement is a Personal Service Contract between the City and the Employee.

C. This Agreement shall commence and become effective as of (date).
D. If any provision, or any portion thereof, contained in this Agreement is held to be unconstitutional, invalid, or unenforceable, the remainder of this Agreement, or any portion thereof, shall be deemed severable and shall not be affected and remain in full force and effect.

F. If any dispute arises regarding the terms or conditions of this agreement, the parties agree to have said dispute resolved through arbitration, by a mutually selected arbitrator through the American Arbitration Association (AAA).

SECTION 13. RESIDENCY

At all times during the term of this Agreement, the Employee shall live and reside in the City of [Name].

SECTION 14. DISABILITY

Notwithstanding anything to the contrary contained in this Agreement, if the Employee becomes permanently or partially disabled to the extent that he/she cannot perform the essential functions of the position, with or without a reasonable accommodation, the City, shall have the right to terminate this Agreement.

SECTION 15. GOVERNING LAW

This Agreement shall be governed by the laws of the State of (STATE).

IN WITNESS WHEREOF, the City has caused this Agreement to be signed and executed in its behalf by its Mayor (Mayor), and the Employee has signed and executed this Agreement, in duplicate, the day and year first above written.

In the presence of:

CITY

_____
Mayor

EMPLOYEE

_____
Chief

Letter of Agreement—Example 8

[Date]

Mr. John Doe
Street Address
City, State Zip

Dear Mr. Doe:

The city of XXX is pleased that you have accepted the position of police chief. The purpose of this letter is to advise you of those major employment issues that are a condition of your job acceptance.

As has been agreed, you will begin employment with the city of XXX on [Date]. Your annual salary will be $60,000, and the city will contribute an amount equal to 7 percent of your salary to the ICMA deferred compensation plan in lieu of pension payments.

You will be provided with a fully insured vehicle that can be used for personal business and by family members. The vehicle will be installed with a cellular telephone at city expense.

The city will reimburse you for all reasonable moving expenses, and you and your spouse will be provided with airfare and accommodations for two househunting trips. Once you have purchased a home in XXX, you will receive a mortgage reimbursement equal to your monthly mortgage payments in XYZ or a monthly allocation of $700, whichever is less, until you sell your XYZ home, for a period not to exceed one year.

You will be credited with 15 days vacation and 45 days sick leave. You will earn vacation at the rate of 15 days per year and sick leave at a rate of 12 days per year. In addition to the customary life insurance coverage for other employees, you will receive an additional $100,000 term life insurance coverage.

All of your business and civic organization membership expenses will be reimbursed by the city, and it is understood that you will, at a minimum and on an annual basis, be authorized and funded to attend the International Association of Chiefs of Police conference, the Police Executive Research Forum's Annual Meeting, the state police chief conference, and one other out-of-state meeting or training program.

Sincerely,

(name)
City Manager

Appendix G

H   Suggested Reading List

American Bar Association Project on Standards for Criminal Justice (1973). *Standards Relating to the Urban Police Function*. New York: American Bar Association.

Banton, Michael P. (1964). *The Policeman in the Community*. London: Tavistock.

Bayley, David H. and Egon Bittner. (1989). Learning the Skills of Policing. In *Critical Issues in Policing: Contemporary Readings*, edited by Roger G. Dunham and Geoffrey P. Alpert. Prospect Heights, Ill.: Waveland.

Bittner, Egon (1970). *The Functions of the Police in Modern Society*. Chevy Chase, Md.: National Institute of Mental Health.

Clarke, Ronald V.G. (1997). *Situational Crime Prevention: Successful Case Studies*. 2nd Edition. Albany, N.Y.: Harrow & Heston.

Delattre, Edwin J. (1996). *Character and Cops*. 3rd Edition. Washington, D.C.: American Enterprise Institute Press.

Eck, John E. and William Spelman (1987). *Problem Solving: Problem-Oriented Policing in Newport News*. Washington, D.C.: Police Executive Research Forum.

Fogelson, Robert M. (1977). *Big City Police*. Cambridge, Mass.: Harvard University Press.

Geller, William (1995). *Managing Innovation*. Washington, D.C.: Police Executive Research Forum.

Geller, William (1992). *Deadly Force: What We Know*. Washington, D.C.: Police Executive Research Forum.

Geller, William (ed.) (1991). *Local Government Police Management*. 3rd Edition. Washington, D.C.: International City/County Management Association.

Goldstein, Herman (1990). *Problem-Oriented Policing*. New York: McGraw-Hill.

Goldstein, Herman (1979). Improving Policing: A Problem-Oriented Approach. *Crime and Delinquency* 25:236–258

Goldstein, Herman (1975). *Policing a Free Society*. Cambridge, Mass.: Ballinger.

Kelling, George L. with Catherine M. Coles (1995). *Fixing Broken Windows: Restoring Order in American Cities*. Westport, Conn.: Praeger.

Kelling, George L. and Mark H. Moore (1988). The Evolving Strategy of Policing. In *Perspectives on Policing*. Rockville, Md.: National Institute of Justice.

Kelling, George L., Anthony M. Pate, Duane Dieckman and Charles E. Brown (1974). *The Kansas City Preventive Patrol Experiment: A Summary Report*. Washington, D.C.: Police Foundation.

Kerner Commission (1968). *Report of the National Advisory Commission on Civil Disorders*. Washington, D.C.: U.S. Government Printing Office.

Klockars, Carl B. (1985). *The Idea of Police*. Thousand Oaks, Calif.: Sage Publications.

LaFave, Wayne R. (1965). *Arrest: The Decision to Take a Suspect into Custody*. Boston: Little Brown.

Manning, Peter K. (1997). *Police Work: The Social Organization of Policing*. 2nd Edition. Prospect, Ill.: Waveland.

Marx, Gary T. (1988). *Undercover: Police Surveillance in America*. Berkeley, Calif.: University of California Press.

Monkkonen, Eric H. (1981). *Police in Urban America, 1860–1920*. New York: Cambridge University Press.

Morris, Norval and Michael Tonry (eds.) (1992). *Modern Policing*. Chicago: University of Chicago.

Muir, William Ker, Jr. (1977). *Police: Streetcorner Politicians*. Chicago: University of Chicago Press.

National Commission on Law Observance and Enforcement (1931). Report on Police. *The Wickersham Report*. Washington, D.C.: U.S. Government Printing Office.

Punch, Maurice, (ed.) (1983). *Control in the Police Organization*. Cambridge, Mass.: MIT Press.

Reiner, Robert (1992). *The Politics of Police*. Toronto: University of Toronto Press.

Reiss, Albert J., Jr. and Jeffrey A. Roth, (eds.) (1993). *Understanding and Preventing Violence*. Washington, D.C.: National Academy Press.

Reiss, Albert J., Jr. (1971). *The Police and the Public*. New Haven, Conn.: Yale University.

Reuss-Ianni, Elizabeth (1983). *The Two Cultures of Policing: Street Cops and Management Cops*. New Brunswick, N.J.: Transaction Books.

Rubinstein, Jonathon (1973). *City Police*. New York: Farrar, Straus & Giroux.

Sherman, Lawrence et al. (1998), *Preventing Crime: What Works, What Doesn't, What's Promising*. Washington, D.C.: National Institute of Justice.

Skogan, Wesley G. (1990). *Disorder and Decline: Crime and the Spiral of Decay in America's Neighborhoods*. Berkeley, Calif.: University of California Press.

Skolnick, Jerome H. (1966). *Justice Without Trial: Law Enforcement in Democratic Society*. 3rd Edition. New York: MacMillan.

Sparrow, Malcolm K., Mark H. Moore and David M. Kennedy (1990). *Beyond 911: A New Era for Policing*. New York: Basic Books.

The President's Commission on Law Enforcement and the Administration of Justice (1967). *Task Force Report: The Police*. Washington, D.C.: U.S. Government Printing Office.

Trojanowicz, Robert and Bonnie Bucqueroux (1998). *Community Policing: A Contemporary Perspective*. 2nd Edition. Cincinnati: Anderson.

Van Maanen, John (1974). Working the Street: A Developmental View of Police Behavior. In *The Potential for Reform of Criminal Justice,* edited by Herbert Jacob. Beverly Hills, Calif.: Sage.

Vollmer, August (1969). *The Police and Modern Society*. College Park, Md.: McGrath.

Walker, Samuel (1999). *The Police in America: An Introduction*. Boston: McGraw-Hill.

Walker, Samuel A. (1977). *A Critical History of Police Reform: The Emergence of Professionalism*. Lexington, Mass.: Lexington Books.

Wasserman, Robert and Mark H. Moore (1988). Values in Policing. *Perspectives on Policing*. Washington, D.C.: National Institute of Justice and Harvard University.

Westley, William A. (1970). *Violence and the Police: A Sociological Study of Law, Custom and Morality*. Cambridge, Mass.: MIT Press.

Wilson, James Q., and George L. Kelling (1989). Making Neighborhoods Safe. *The Atlantic Monthly* February:46-52.

Wilson, James Q., and George L. Kelling (1982). Broken Windows: The Police and Neighborhood Safety. *The Atlantic Monthly* March:29–38.

Wilson, James Q. (1985). *Thinking About Crime*. Rev. Edition. New York: Vintage

Wilson, James Q. (1968). *Varieties of Police Behavior: The Management of Law and Order in Eight Communities*. Cambridge, Mass.: Harvard University Press.

PERF DISTRIBUTED the following survey to 518 U.S. city and county police chiefs and other non-elected law enforcement agency directors policing jurisdictions, all with populations of approximately 50,000 or more. After the initial September 1997 mailing and a follow-up mailing, 358 valid responses were received.

For most of the questions listed below, the total number of respondents who answered in the affirmative and the corresponding percentage are provided.

Selection Process

Values	Frequency	Percentage

1. How many years of police experience did you have prior to your first job as chief?

a. _____ years of sworn experience [Answers rounded off to nearest year]

	Frequency	Percentage
Between 1 and 5 years	6	1.7%
Between 6 and 10 years	16	4.5%
Between 11 and 15 years	37	10.3%
Between 16 and 20 years	103	28.8%
More than 20 years	192	53.6%
No answer	4	1.1%

b. _____ years of non-sworn experience

	Frequency	Percentage
Zero years	56	15.6%
Between 1 and 5 years	38	10.6%
Between 6 and 10 years	8	2.2%
Between 11 and 20 years	0	0.0%
More than 20 years	1	0.3%
No answer	255	71.2%

2. How many times have you applied for a police chief's job?_____ times

Between 0 and 1 times	170	47.5%
Between 2 and 5 times	133	37.2%
Between 6 and 10 times	28	7.8%
Between 11 and 15 times	8	2.2%
Between 16 and 20 times	3	0.8%
More than 20 times	6	1.7%
No answer	10	2.8%

3. How did you obtain your current position?

Promoted from within department	203	56.7%
Appointed from outside department	151	42.2%
Appointed from outside department (but with prior experience in department)	2	0.6%
No answer	2	0.6%

4. What was your immediate previous position/rank_____

Patrol Officer	1	0.3%
Sergeant	8	2.2%
Lieutenant	24	6.7%
Captain/Commander	99	27.6%
Major	16	4.5%
Detective/Investigator	7	2.0%
Assistant Chief/Deputy	121	33.8%
Chief	58	16.2%
City Official	1	0.3%
Other	21	5.9%
No answer	2	0.6%

How long did you hold your previous position/rank?_____

Less than one year	10	2.8%
1–2 years	77	21.5%
3–5 years	127	35.5%
6–10 years	99	27.6%
More than 10 years	29	8.1%
No answer	16	4.5%

5. By whom was the search for your current position conducted? Check all that apply:

City/county manager	137	38.3%
Police commission	27	7.5%
Ad hoc committee	40	11.2%
Private executive search firm	67	18.7%
National police organization (PERF, IACP, etc.)	26	7.3%
Mayor	80	22.3%
Other_____	41	11.4%
No answer	3	0.8%

6. How was the search/hiring conducted? Check all that apply:

Candidates within agency considered	303	84.6%
Candidates outside agency considered	212	59.2%
Civil service examination	56	15.6%
National search	161	45.0%
Assessment center utilized	78	21.8%
Community input	148	41.3%
Other_____	64	17.9%
No answer	6	1.7%

7. Who is your supervisor? Check all that apply:

City manager/administrator	204	57.0%
County manager/administrator	11	3.1%
Mayor	118	33.0%
Elected board	21	5.9%
Police commission	20	5.6%
Other_____	31	8.7%
No answer	2	0.6%

8. Who appointed you? Check all that apply:

City manager/administrator	181	50.6%
County manager/administrator	7	2.0%
Mayor	128	35.8%
Elected board	42	11.7%
Police commission	17	4.7%
Other_____	28	7.8%
No answer	3	0.8%

9. Is your performance formally evaluated by your supervisor?

Yes	247	69.0%
No	104	29.1%
No answer	7	2.0%

If yes, how often? _____

4 times per year	4	1.1%
2 times per year	18	5.0%
1 time per year	192	53.6%
1 time every 2 years	1	0.3%
1 time every 3 or more years	2	0.6%
Not applicable/No answer	141	39.4%

10. Does your employer require you to submit to the following on an annual basis?

Medical exam?

Yes	56	15.6%
No	291	81.3%
No answer	11	3.1%

Physical fitness exam?

Yes	26	7.3%
No	310	86.6%
No answer	22	6.1%

Psychological evaluation?

Yes	2	0.6%
No	327	91.3%
No answer	29	8.1%

Drug testing?

Yes	71	19.8%
No	276	77.1%
No answer	11	3.1%

Polygraph?

Yes	1	0.3%
No	327	91.3%
No answer	30	8.4%

11. Did your employer require you to submit to the following as a condition of employment?

Medical exam?

Yes	185	51.7%
No	159	44.4%
No answer	14	3.9%

Physical fitness exam?

Yes	83	23.2%
No	234	65.4%
No answer	41	11.5%

Psychological evaluation?

Yes	118	33.0%
No	205	57.3%
No answer	35	9.8%

Drug testing?

Yes	146	40.8%
No	186	52.0%
No answer	26	7.3%

Polygraph?

Yes	30	8.4%
No	284	79.3%
No answer	44	12.3%

12. Does your agency conduct random drug testing of employees?

Yes	163	45.5%
No	191	53.4%
No answer	4	1.1%

If yes, are you subject to being tested?

Yes	145	40.5%
No	15	4.2%
Not applicable/No answer	198	55.3%

13. Check the five most significant factors that influenced you to leave your last position:

Career advancement/promotion	228	63.7%
Desire for a greater challenge	220	61.5%
Salary/benefit considerations	178	49.7%
Other_____	91	25.4%
Consideration of family members	88	24.6%
Became eligible for pension	63	17.6%
Lack of budgetary resources	38	10.6%
Boredom	35	9.8%
Political/social community climate (i.e., too liberal/conservative)	27	7.5%
Poor chemistry between you and government official(s)	26	7.3%
Pressure from a higher authority	16	4.5%
Pressure from interest groups	13	3.6%
Misconduct/corruption/scandal involving agency personnel	10	2.8%
Lack of community support	9	2.5%
Racial conflict(s) within the community	6	1.7%
High/rising level of crime	5	1.4%
Racial conflict(s) within the department	5	1.4%
Media pressure	2	0.6%
No answer	49	13.7%

14. Check the five most significant factors that influenced you to accept your current position:

Career advancement/promotion	302	84.4%
Desire for a greater challenge	299	83.5%
Salary/benefit considerations	247	69.0%
Consideration of family members	139	38.8%
Political/social community climate (i.e., too liberal/conservative)	95	26.5%
Other_____	78	21.8%
Became eligible for pension	41	11.5%
High/rising level of crime	22	6.1%
Misconduct/corruption/scandal involving agency personnel	19	5.3%
Pressure from a higher authority	19	5.3%
Pressure from interest groups	16	4.5%
Racial conflict(s) within the community	15	4.2%

Boredom	10	2.8%
Lack of community support	9	2.5%
Poor chemistry between you and government official(s)	9	2.5%
Racial conflict(s) within the department	8	2.2%
Lack of budgetary resources	6	1.7%
Media pressure	1	0.3%
No answer	11	3.1%

15. **What were the personal/professional attributes that led to your hiring as chief in your current jurisdiction? (i.e., What made you the most qualified? What did the hiring authority like about you?)

See Chapter 11 for selected responses.

Benefits

18. Do you have a contract/employment agreement?

Yes	95	26.5%
No	262	73.2%
No answer	1	0.3%

If yes, what is the specified length of the contract? _____

Less than 1 year	1	0.3%
1–2 years	10	2.8%
3–5 years	33	9.2%
6–10 years	4	1.1%
More than 10 years	2	0.6%
Other (e.g., open-ended)	31	8.7%
Not applicable/No answer	277	77.4%

21. Which type of pension program do you have through your employer?

Defined benefit plan (guaranteed payment based on percentage of salary)	252	70.4%
Choose one:		
a. _____ State plan	213	59.5%
b. _____ Local plan	95	26.5%
c. _____ Both state and local plan	7	2.0%
d. _____ Not applicable/No answer	43	12.0%

Defined contribution plan
(variable payment based on investment
return and employer/employee
contributions, i.e., 457, 401K, 403, etc.) 41   11.5%
Both defined benefit and contribution plan 58   16.2%
No answer   7   2.0%

22. Is your pension program portable?
Yes   183   51.1%
No   164   45.8%
No answer   11   3.1%

If yes, is the program transferable out of state?
Yes   37   10.3%
No   141   39.4%
Not applicable/No answer   180   50.3%

23. How many years of service are required for 100% retirement vesting?
_____ years
Zero years   11   3.1%
1–5 years   49   13.7%
6–10 years   68   19.0%
11–15 years   6   1.7%
16–20 years   54   15.1%
More than 20 years   116   32.4%
No answer   54   15.1%

24. Do you think the terms of your pension plan restrict your professional mobility?
Yes   139   38.8%
No   215   60.1%
No answer   4   1.1%

25. Is there a mandatory retirement age for your current position?
Yes   82   22.9%
No   272   76.0%
No answer   4   1.1%

If yes, what is the age? _____ years old

50	1	0.3%
55	2	0.6%
56–60	7	2.0%
61–64	5	1.4%
65	52	14.5%
Over 65	14	3.9%
Not applicable/No answer	277	77.4%

27. Are you eligible for incentive bonuses?

Yes	75	20.9%
No	280	78.2%
No answer	3	0.8%

28. Check all of the following that are included in your benefits package:

Health insurance	350	97.8%
Professional liability insurance	166	46.4%
Dental insurance	297	83.0%
Deferred retirement	104	29.1%
Deferred compensation	245	68.4%
Life insurance	327	91.3%
Vision care insurance	205	57.3%
Compensatory time	123	34.4%
No answer	4	1.1%

29. On employment with your current agency, which one of the following did you accept?

Standard employee benefits package	267	74.6%
Customized benefits package	78	21.8%
Both standard and customized benefits package	4	1.1%
No answer	9	2.5%

30. For which of the following expenditures do you receive reimbursement from your employer?

Membership fees for professional organizations?

Yes	339	94.7%
No	16	4.5%
No answer	3	0.8%

Travel expenses for professional conferences?

Yes	347	96.9%
No	9	2.5%
No answer	2	0.6%

Business related luncheon/dinner meetings?

Yes	258	72.1%
No	91	25.4%
No answer	9	2.5%

Professional subscriptions?

Yes	341	95.3%
No	13	3.6%
No answer	4	1.1%

Moving expenses when hired?

Yes	111	31.0%
No	188	52.5%
No answer	59	16.5%

Executive development programs?

Yes	323	90.2%
No	29	8.1%
No answer	6	1.7%

31. What provisions have been made for your business automobile? Check all that apply:

Automobile included in benefits package?

Yes	253	70.7%
No	41	11.5%
No answer	64	17.9%

Employer leases a vehicle (employer selects vehicle make)?

Yes	15	4.2%
No	138	38.5%
No answer	205	57.3%

Employer leases a vehicle (employee selects vehicle make)?

Yes	24	6.7%
No	130	36.3%
No answer	204	57.0%

May use employer-owned vehicle for business only?

Yes	103	28.8%
No	79	22.1%
No answer	176	49.2%

May use employer-owned vehicle for business and personal use?

Yes	199	55.6%
No	64	17.9%
No answer	95	26.5%

32. What is your current annual base salary (pre-tax)? $_____

$25,000–$50,000	8	2.2%
$50,001–$60,000	2	15.9%
$60,001–$65,000	17	4.7%
$65,001–$70,000	24	6.7%
$70,001–$75,000	41	11.5%
$75,001–$80,000	29	8.1%
$80,001–$85,000	32	8.9%
$85,001–$90,000	36	10.1%
$90,001–$95,000	29	8.1%
$95,001–$100,000	19	5.3%
$100,001–$120,000	69	19.3%
More than $120,000	21	5.9%
No answer	12	3.4%

Agency Data

33. In what state do you hold your current position? _____

State	Count	Percent
Alabama	4	1.1%
Alaska	1	0.3%
Arizona	8	2.2%
Arkansas	3	0.8%
California	52	14.5%
Colorado	8	2.2%
Connecticut	12	3.4%
Florida	28	7.8%
Georgia	8	2.2%
Hawaii	3	0.8%
Illinois	11	3.1%
Indiana	9	2.5%
Iowa	4	1.1%
Kansas	5	1.4%
Kentucky	4	1.1%
Louisiana	5	1.4%
Maryland	5	1.4%
Massachusetts	16	4.5%
Michigan	12	3.4%
Minnesota	4	1.1%
Mississippi	2	0.6%
Missouri	4	1.1%
Montana	1	0.3%
Nebraska	1	0.3%
Nevada	3	0.8%
New Hampshire	2	0.6%
New Jersey	19	5.3%
New Mexico	2	0.6%
New York	19	5.3%
North Carolina	10	2.8%
Ohio	10	2.8%
Oklahoma	3	0.8%
Oregon	4	1.1%
Pennsylvania	7	2.0%
Rhode Island	3	0.8%
South Carolina	4	1.1%
Tenneseee	6	1.7%
Texas	32	8.9%

Utah	2	0.6%
Virginia	10	2.8%
Washington	5	1.4%
West Virginia	1	0.3%
Wisconsin	3	0.8%
No answer	3	0.8%

34. Approximately how many of the following personnel are in your agency?

full-time sworn/commissioned

1–50	2	0.6%
51–100	7	2.0%
101–150	112	31.3%
151–200	82	22.9%
201–250	29	8.1%
251–300	26	7.3%
301–350	9	2.5%
351–400	16	4.5%
401–450	8	2.2%
451–500	7	2.0%
501–1000	32	8.9%
More than 1000	23	6.4%
No answer	5	1.4%

full-time civilian

1–50	131	36.6%
51–100	109	30.4%
101–150	46	12.8%
151–200	16	4.5%
201–250	12	3.4%
251–300	10	2.8%
301–350	6	1.7%
351–400	4	1.1%
More than 400	15	4.2%
No answer	9	2.5%

35. What is the population of the jurisdiction in which you serve?

49,000 or less	23	6.4%
50,000–75,000	76	21.2%
75,001–100,000	79	22.1%
100,001–150,000	70	19.6%
150,001–200,000	40	11.2%
200,001–250,000	12	3.4%
250,001–300,000	10	2.8%
300,001–500,000	18	5.0%
500,001–1,000,000	14	3.9%
More than 1,000,000	8	2.2%
No answer	8	2.2%

36. What is the form of government in your jurisdiction? Check all that apply:

City manager/administrator	194	54.2%
County manager/administrator	14	3.9%
Mayor	180	50.3%
Board of police commissioners	13	3.6%
Alderman	24	6.7%
City board of supervisors		
____Elected	44	12.3%
____Appointed	41	11.5%
County board of supervisors		
____Elected	11	3.1%
____Appointed	10	2.8%
Other_____	53	14.8%
No answer	2	0.6%

INDIVIDUAL DATA

38. What is your race?

Asian	3	0.8%
Caucasian	292	81.6%
Hispanic	17	4.7%
African American	39	10.9%
Pacific Islander	1	0.3%
Native American	3	0.8%
Other_____	1	0.3%
No answer	2	0.6%

39. What is your gender?

Male	355	99.2%
Female	2	0.6%
No answer	1	0.3%

40. What is your age?_____ years old

40 or younger	6	1.7%
41–45	49	13.7%
46–50	132	36.9%
51–55	110	30.7%
56–60	38	10.6%
61–65	15	4.2%
Over 65	1	0.3%
No answer	7	2.0%

41. What education have you obtained? Check all that apply:

High school	351	98.0%
A.A.	119	33.2%
B.A./B.S.	312	87.2%
M.A.	166	46.4%
Ph.D.	5	1.4%
J.D.	12	3.4%
Other_____	53	14.8%
No answer	1	0.3%

Six respondents stated that they do not have a high school degree. Each one, however, stated that he or she had obtained some "other" type of degree.

42. If you received a college degree, what was your major? _____

Top Five Degrees:

Criminology/Administration of Justice/ Criminal Justice	154	43.0%
Public policy/Political Science/Government	94	26.3%
Other_____	59	16.5%
Business	28	7.8%
Sociology/Anthropology	20	5.6%

43. What has been your military experience? Check all that apply:

No military experience	141	39.4%
Army	98	27.4%
Air Force	46	12.8%
Coast Guard	4	1.1%
Navy	22	6.1%
Marine Corps	29	8.1%
Other_____	15	4.2%
No answer	1	0.3%

44. Which of the following executive training programs have you attended? Check all that apply:

SMIP/PERF	50	14.0%
LEEDS	101	28.2%
FBI National Academy	180	50.3%
Southern Police Institute	30	8.4%
National Executive Institute	60	16.8%
Northwestern Traffic Institute	30	8.4%
Other_____	94	26.3%
No answer	49	13.7%

45. How many years did your predecessor hold his/her position?
_____ years [Answers rounded off to nearest year]

Less than one year	3	0.8%
1–5 years	181	50.6%
6–10 years	88	24.6%
11–15 years	40	11.2%
16–20 years	23	6.4%
More than 20 years	15	4.2%
No answer	8	2.2%

In jurisdictions with populations of 500,000 or more, the average tenure of predecessors was 4.93.

How many years have you held your current police chief position?
_____ years [Answers rounded off to nearest year]

Less than one year	11	3.1%
1–5 years	216	60.3%
6–10 years	79	22.1%
11–15 years	21	5.9%
16–20 years	10	2.8%
More than 20 years	5	1.4%
No answer	16	4.5%

How many years of experience do you have as a police chief?
_____ years [Answers rounded off to nearest year]

Less than one year	8	2.2%
1–5 years	168	46.9%
6–10 years	93	26.0%
11–15 years	33	9.2%
16–20 years	21	5.9%
More than 20 years	15	4.2%
No answer	20	5.6%

How many years do you plan to remain at your current chief's job?
_____ years [Answers rounded off to nearest year]

Less than one year	9	2.5%
1–5 years	140	39.1%
6–10 years	98	27.4%
11–15 years	16	4.5%
16–20 years	5	1.4%
More than 20 years	1	0.3%
No answer	89	24.9%

46. On an average work week:

Number of hours you work in the office? _____ hours

1–30 hours	70	19.6%
31–40 hours	106	29.6%
41–50 hours	136	38.0%
More than 50 hours	40	11.2%
No answer	6	1.7%

Number of hours you work out of the office (meetings, call-outs, etc.)?
_____ hours

1–10 hours	226	63.1%
11–15 hours	47	13.1%
16–20 hours	52	14.5%
More than 20 hours	26	7.3%
No answer	7	2.0%

Number of hours you work at home? _____ hours

Zero hours	37	10.3%
1–5 hours	161	45.0%
6–10 hours	106	29.6%
11–15 hours	13	3.6%
16–20 hours	7	2.0%
No answer	34	9.5%

47. Which of the following law enforcement publications do you regularly read? Check all that apply:

City and County	120	33.5%
Governing	176	49.2%
Law Enforcement News	199	55.6%
Law and Order	258	72.1%
National League of Cities	164	45.8%
Police	108	30.2%
Police Chief	351	98.0%
Subject to Debate (PERF)	144	40.2%
Other_____	69	19.3%
No answer	4	1.1%

48. Which television programs do you regularly watch? Check all that apply:

Police related		
(*America's Most Wanted, COPS*, etc.)	52	14.5%
National news	307	85.8%
News magazines		
(*20/20, 60 Minutes, Dateline*, etc.)	234	65.4%
Regional news	283	79.1%
CNN	244	68.2%
C-SPAN	70	19.6%
Other_____	38	10.6%
No answer	10	2.8%

49. Which popular press do you regularly read? Check all that apply:

Wall Street Journal	56	15.6%
New York Times	49	13.7%
USA Today	119	33.2%
National daily	42	11.7%
Regional daily	272	76.0%
Newsweek	120	33.5%
Time	67	18.7%
Other_____	60	16.8%
No answer	15	4.2%

50. Do you have e-mail in your office?

Yes	264	73.7%
No	89	24.9%
No answer	5	1.4%

Do you have e-mail in your home?

Yes	151	42.2%
No	194	54.2%
No answer	13	3.6%

51. Do you have Internet access in your office?

Yes	252	70.4%
No	100	27.9%
No answer	6	1.7%

Do you have Internet access in your home?

Yes	167	46.6%
No	179	50.0%
No answer	12	3.4%

52. After you retire, what do you intend to do? Check all that apply:

Private-sector work	117	32.7%
Non police-related work	94	26.3%
Write	58	16.2%
Teach	169	47.2%
Consult	156	43.6%
Full-time leisure	56	15.6%
Other_____	76	21.2%
No answer	13	3.6%

54. If you had it to do over again, would you still aspire to be a police chief?

Yes	311	86.9%
No	30	8.4%
No answer	17	4.7%

55. Which one of the following best describes your overall job satisfaction?

completely satisfied	158	44.1%
somewhat satisfied	177	49.4%
indifferent	3	0.8%
somewhat dissatisfied	9	2.5%
completely dissatisfied	1	0.3%
No answer	10	2.8%

56. What were the most significant experiences/achievements that prepared you for your present position?

See Chapter 11 for selected responses.

59. What advice would you offer to an individual who aspires to a chief's position?

See Chapter 11 for selected responses.

About the Authors

WILLIAM E. KIRCHHOFF is a former city manager with 25 years experience in five communities, ranging in population from 15,000 to 300,000. He was a frequent lecturer on the subject of career advancement before groups sponsored by the International Association of Chiefs of Police, the Police Executive Research Forum, and the International City/County Management Association. He has served on the graduate faculty of five universities, and lectures regularly for the Northwestern University Traffic Institute and the Law Enforcement Management Institute at Sam Houston State University.

Kirchhoff has served three terms on the Commission on Accreditation for Law Enforcement Agencies, and a term on the National Community Oriented Policing Resource Board, and has worked closely with some of the country's leading law enforcement officials.

He is the author of several books including *The Job Hunting Municipal Executive, The Job Hunting Handbook for the Local Government Professional,* and *The Art of War for Public Managers.*

A former commissioned U.S. Army officer, Kirchhoff served in Vietnam and was awarded the Bronze Star.

During his career in city management, Kirchhoff has read thousands of résumés and interviewed several hundred men and women for key management positions. He has employed executive search firms to assist with a variety of searches, including that of police chief. Kirchhoff has hired 10 police chiefs, and has participated in the selection processes of more than 30 police chiefs.

CHARLOTTE LANSINGER has been a specialist in the field of police chief selection for more than 12 years. She has managed police chief selection processes for the Police Executive Research Forum (PERF) since 1993. Before her work for PERF, she was the director of executive search services at the International Association of Chiefs of Police (IACP), where she cofounded the search service with Chuck Wexler.

Lansinger has assisted in the placement of more than 50 police chiefs in communities that range in population from 10,000 to 800,000. She has 16 years of experience in personnel selection and human resources management. Lansinger lectures on police executive selection issues and provides law enforcement career counseling. She has also served as a consultant for the development and administration of various police promotional examinations and assessment centers.

Lansinger holds a bachelor's degree in government and public service from Indiana University of Pennsylvania.

JAMES BURACK is counsel and director of operations, and an associate in executive search services, for the Police Executive Research Forum (PERF). He has assisted with executive searches in a variety of jurisdictions. He has also been heavily involved in various aspects of PERF's work in problem-oriented policing (POP), and worked extensively on international policing projects, incuding Bosnia, for the U.S. State Department and Department of Justice.

A U.S. Marine Corps major, he has served as a military prosecutor and Special Assistant U.S. Attorney in Southern California, and as a civil affairs officer in Kosovo.

Burack was a police officer with the Westminster (Colorado) Police Department.

He received a bachelor's degree in government and history from Dartmouth College, and earned a law degree from the University of Colorado. He is a member of the bar in California, Colorado, and the District of Columbia.

About PERF

THE POLICE EXECUTIVE RESEARCH FORUM (PERF) is a national professional association of chief executives of large city, county and state law enforcement agencies. PERF's objective is to improve the delivery of police services and the effectiveness of crime control through several means:

1. the exercise of strong national leadership,

2. the public debate of police and criminal issues,

3. the development of research and policy, and

4. the provision of vital management and leadership services to police agencies.

PERF members are selected on the basis of their commitment to PERF's objectives and principles. PERF operates under the following tenets:

1. Research, experimentation and exchange of ideas through public discussion and debate are paths for the development of a comprehensive body of knowledge about policing.

2. Substantial and purposeful academic study is a prerequisite for acquiring, understanding and adding to that body of knowledge.

3. Maintenance of the highest standards of ethics and integrity is imperative in the improvement of policing.

4. The police must, within the limits of the law, be responsible and accountable to citizens as the ultimate source of police authority.

5. The principles embodied in the Constitution are the foundation of policing.